# ReUrbano

## Toward a City

# Contents

# A Book

Alberto Kritzler
and Rodrigo Rivero Borrell

The following pages tell part of the story of "city-making" from the perspective of a laboratory working to make a positive impact on the city—succeeding on occasion and at other times learning, building, changing, or inspiring. Each project is the product of a collaboration, with the contrasting visions, disciplines, and proposals of citizens we choose to make a change through conscious real-estate development. Investments in neighborhoods rescue pre-existing urban treasures, always seeking out maximum recycling and regeneration potential, creating heritage value, and recognizing the opportunities offered by Mexico City.

We decided to publish this book as an invitation, or perhaps a provocation, for readers to reflect, participate, and enter the conversation as fellow citizens. What can or should we do in order to improve the city? What spaces of dialogue and construction do we need? How can we create a philosophy where "city-making" is a collaborative exercise that goes beyond urban development? How do we lay the foundations for the wellbeing of future generations?

The book marks ReUrbano's tenth anniversary year: it displays our working processes to give a glimpse of what happens under the surface of our projects. We describe a series of exercises that show the clear difference between having good intentions and turning them into livable realities to enrich communities. By developing architectural and urban projects we conceive how each action has a knock-on effect on the lives of people living in the city.

This book is for us, for our neighbors, for everyone with whom we have worked and collaborated, and for anyone who understands the co-responsibility of all those committed to development—or conscious citizen participation—to make a better city.

# A Commitment to the City

| | |
|---|---|
| Colonia Polanco | Colonia Centro |
| Colonia Juárez | Colonia Tacubaya |
| Colonia Roma | Colonia Escandón |
| Colonia Condesa | Colonia Doctores |

How did ReUrbano start out, and what is behind the name? How did you decide to work together? Why do you work as a real-estate developer? What led you to collaborate with various architecture firms as well as others working in the development sector? What are the challenges of real-estate development and building regulations? How do projects support or create communities? What have you learned in your experience as developers? Where do you see yourselves in ten years' time?

*Alberto Kritzler and Rodrigo Rivero Borrell began collaborating after they identified a shared interest in rescuing derelict buildings possessing histories and architectural qualities with recycling potential. In this way they are working toward making a better city, one that is more alive, active, diverse, and mixed. The commitment to the city is an integral part of each exercise, interconnecting the projects themselves and also linking them to other kinds of urban infrastructure. ReUrbano's approach always differs from other, purely market-driven real-estate development models.*

**RODRIGO RIVERO BORRELL** I like the word "laboratory" because we are researchers in the area of regulations. Listed buildings attract us for their own value but also because they are the only way to build in the kind of city that we hope to create because, to give one example, these projects are exempt from the requirement to incorporate parking spaces. As part of what we call a "laboratory" model we found a subcategory and straight away we requested an exemption from the parking-space requirement. In this way we took advantage of regulations for our own benefit. Our idea was to create an ideological, research-based laboratory with the clear intention to make an impact on neighborhoods.

**ALBERTO KRITZLER** And this is exactly what real-estate development should be about, and that explains our name. The developer is like a cook who adds all kinds of ingredients, yet at the end of the process it is not obvious what has gone into the dish. Or like an orchestra conductor who produces the right sounds at the right time. However, you can debase developments by abusing that power. We cannot ignore the many bad examples of real-estate investors, or the fact that developers make the largest impact on the city, for good or ill. This has given real-estate developments a bad name. But how did we get there?

**RRB** Because of a clear dynamic of mistrust and abuse. Real-estate developers require certain values to integrate their projects within a city, and be aware that they operate both at an urban and a social level.

**AK** That is exactly why we need to bring on board the local community, residents and businesses alike. This is the only way to weave together a city and perform a function that is normally the preserve of the government authorities, because we share that responsibility. We must consider the impact of everything we do and act accordingly.

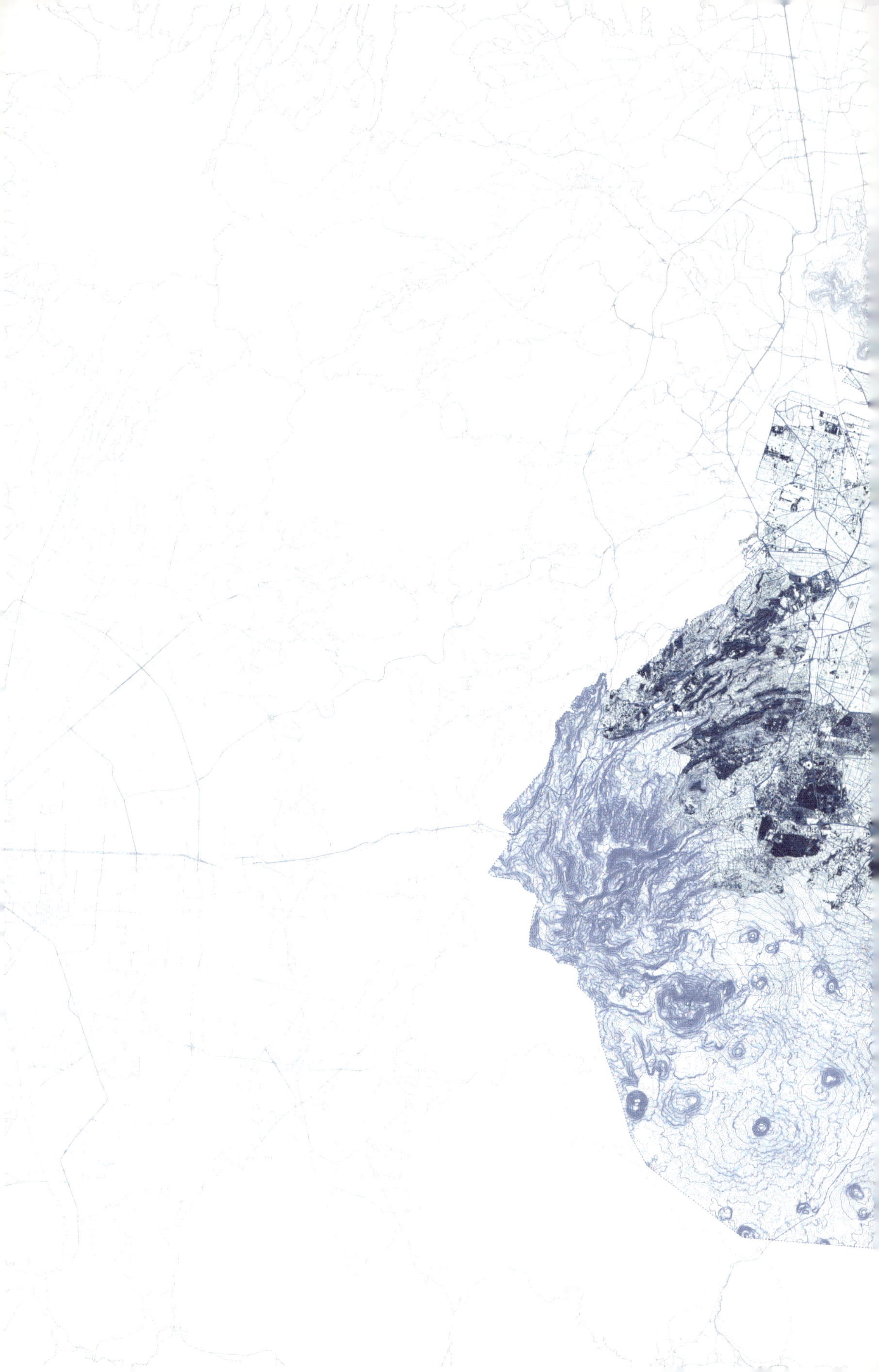

**RRB** In response to the question about the idea behind ReUrbano, I'd answer we were interested in rescuing properties to create a much friendlier and more livable city.

**AK** We've always wanted to rescue derelict buildings to improve the city, reflecting on how to reconfigure dilapidated buildings. We are also interested in being efficient and aware of the resources already used by others, in the city itself, and in the environment.

**RRB** In fact, the prefix "re" denotes recycling, rescuing, but always within a pre-existing urban context. The group's name had to be clear and direct, and we needed to act congruently with it. I've always been uncomfortable with waste, and wasted space. From the outset our focus has been on avoiding waste. Our search for pre-existing constructions led us to develop a partnership. Alberto and I shared similar concerns and our partnership did not evolve into an architecture studio but a real-estate development company.

**AK** The power of action and implementation meant we did not simply want to come up with good ideas but find ways to make them happen. The right vehicle for this turned out to a real-estate development company focused on the urban environment. Our strength lay in the fact we raised our own resources, chose properties ignored by others, and started a new conversation for the city. This happened with Havre 83, a project that taught us how to preserve a building and make it profitable at the same time. It was about proving that the market would rally behind this kind of building if we could highlight a different set of values.

Neighborhood boundaries
Radius of influence
ReUrbano projects
Urban equipment and heritage
Neighborhood buildings
Green areas
Streets
Main avenues
Metrobús stations
Metro stations
Cycle lanes

0
300

1938
EL CAFETO

RESTAURANTE

PARADISET

LA EUROPEA

**RRB** The Havre project represented a complete business operation. We drew up the blueprints, made the purchase, carried out the building work, and handled the sales. We learn something from every experience, and with this project we realized that it was better to bring specialists on board, people who add value in specific areas. Architects need to dedicate all their time to design, and we had to spend our days coordinating everything. I don't think that this means we aren't working as architects but by taking this approach perhaps we could have a greater influence and achieve what we wanted.

**AK** The most enjoyable part of the process is still actually carrying out the project. Getting stuck into every project and working with different architects means that we don't become too attached to our ideas.

**RRB** That's definitely the best part, because some of the other stages require more patience and effort. The biggest challenge today is the regulatory framework (perhaps the project management too). Our dealings with government regulations largely depend on political will and capability. During the first six years we were able to work almost unimpeded, with the technical processes flowing smoothly, but this gradually began to disappear in the run-up to the 2018 elections. It seemed that no-one did anything any more or wanted to give permits. This completely changed our way of working. That's why regulations still pose the greatest challenge; faced with apathetic local authorities that are unwilling to help, patience and perseverance become vital while remaining in close contact with the government offices.

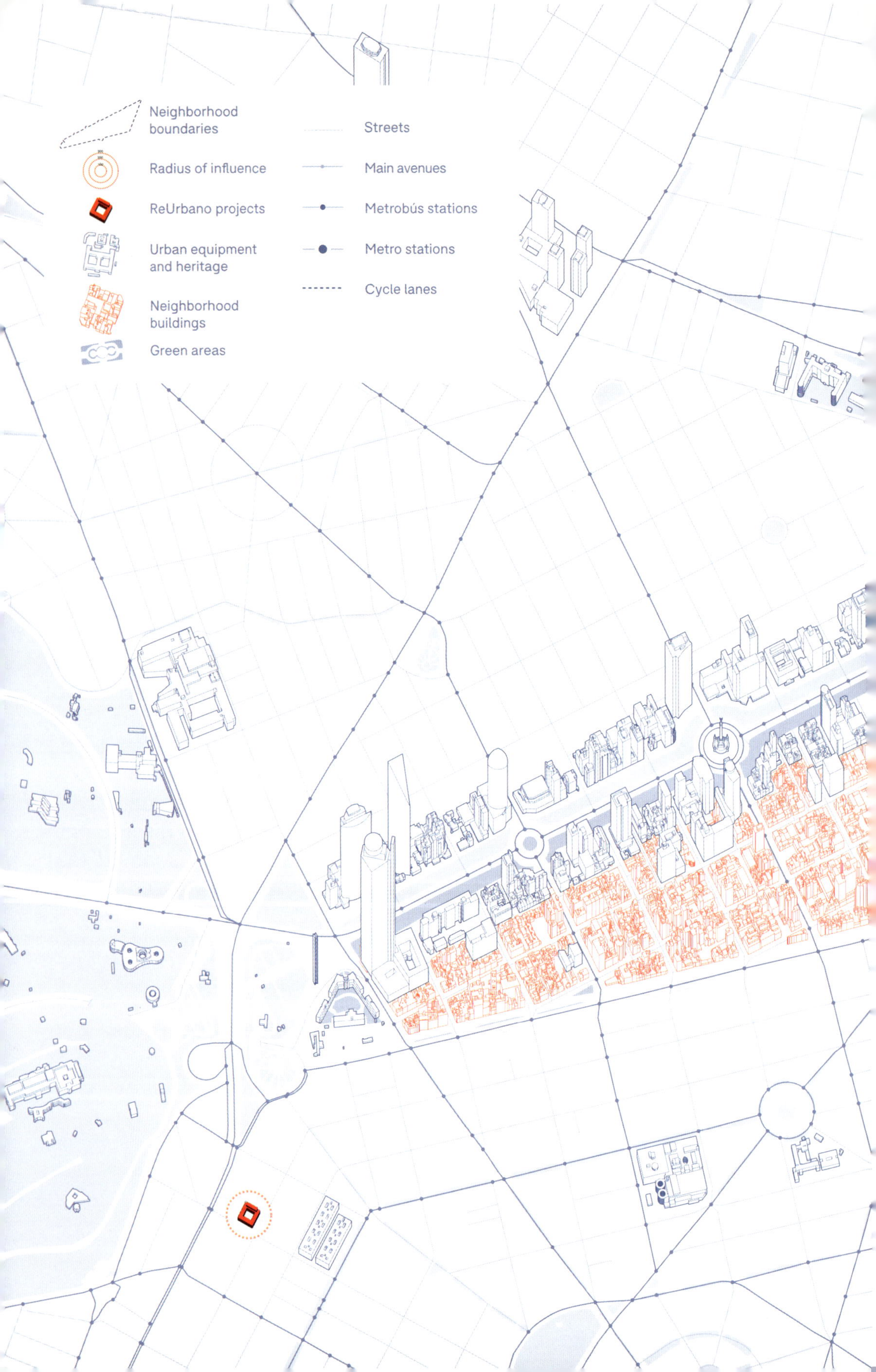

Neighborhood boundaries
Radius of influence
ReUrbano projects
Urban equipment and heritage
Neighborhood buildings
Green areas
Streets
Main avenues
Metrobús stations
Metro stations
Cycle lanes

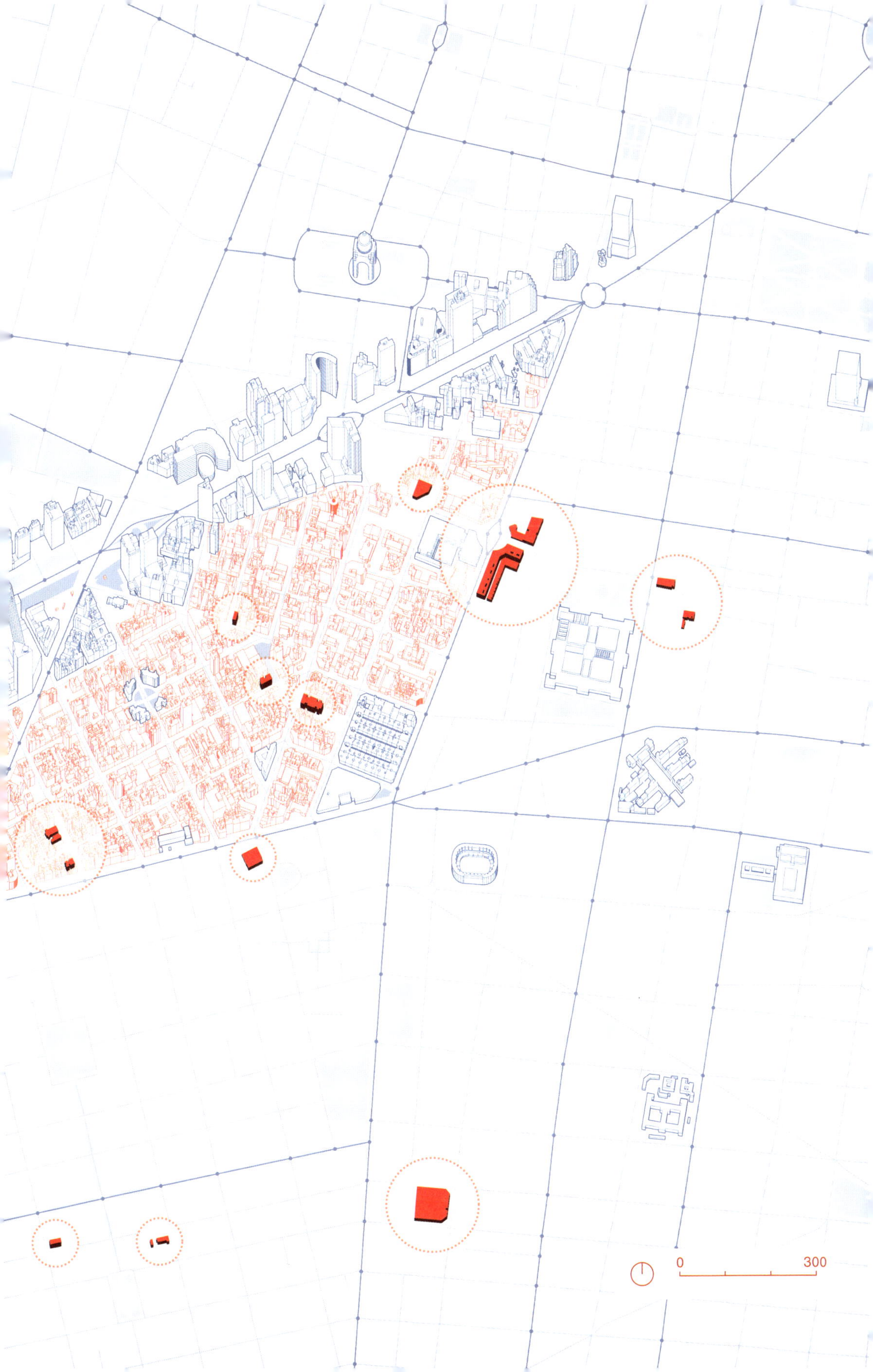
0
300

Mi Socio

PANADERÍA
73

¡POR UN FUTURO FRATERNO Y SOLIDARIO!

HELADERÍA CASA

INTERNET MI ESP@CIO
SOPORTE ◆ SCANNER ◆ IMPRESIONES
CONSUMIBLES ◆ TELEFONO ◆ FAX
INTERNET

CLUB DE CICLISMO

MERCADO
JUÁREZ

TierrAdentro

3A

**AK** Investors also need to be patient. It's a constant search for balance. I think that we are ultimately aware that there are different ways to approach the issue of regulations, and one strategy is to push the law to the limit in order to prove that some changes are indeed possible and beneficial. The Chihuahua project shows that three uses are possible, a system that now works perfectly for the building's residents, the neighborhood, and the city.

**RRB** In this sense, I think that resolving the car issue is one of the greatest achievements of this laboratory. Previously it was unusual for people to invest in properties without parking spaces, but we proved that the market was indeed ready for change. Many people were looking to live closer to their workplace, to save time and improve their quality of life. Our projects sought to encourage a different and desirable lifestyle that prioritized other means of transport, thus improving the environment and building communities.

**AK** From another perspective, we have made an impact in three areas: health, community, and harmony. We avoided naïve romanticism but focused on logical and efficient solutions, respecting the city, because this kind of project increases a sense of harmony and community.

**RRB** Chihuahua is one example of such an improvement. The owner told us that they wanted to help us with the project. They wanted to preserve the façade and leave the parking spaces on the ground floor. We showed that creating a public space has enormous potential, and we achieved this by creating a patio shared by all of the building's residents. We put the shop on the ground floor and the upper floors were used for offices, apartments, and a roof garden. The idea was to prove that such projects could benefit all the stakeholders: owners, residents, and neighbors.

Neighborhood boundaries
Radius of influence
ReUrbano projects
Urban equipment and heritage
Neighborhood buildings
Green areas
Streets
Main avenues
Metrobús stations
Metro stations
Cycle lanes

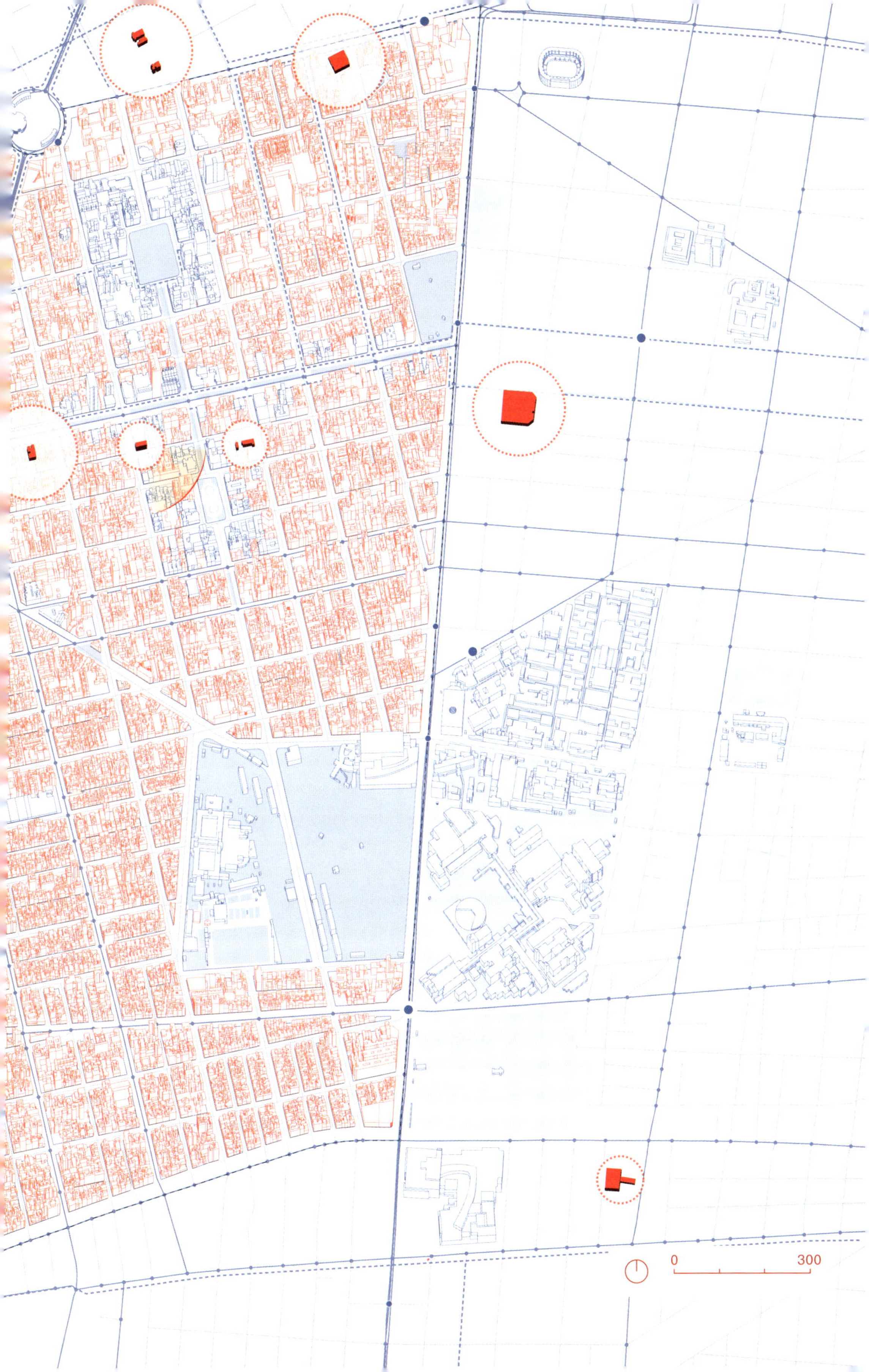

0
300

LIBRERIA
118
LIBRERIA
ATICO

FOREVER

EXPOSICIÓN
GOLES Y PASIONES

**AK** We have both lived in Mexico City and are deeply committed as citizens, ones who have also lived in many other cities around the world such as Barcelona, San Francisco, and New York. I think that our process is mainly about the belief about how we like to live and this is based on our personal experiences. This makes it difficult to explain why we opted for one model instead of another; we find it easier to make the building rather than explain the vision and to persuade others. We like to imagine a life without a car, living alongside strangers we meet on the street each day; that is what creates a community we can belong to, a world where we can live as citizens. Therefore the communal spaces in our projects begin in the street, because the street can always be reinvented and offers infinite possibilities. And although we don't have a perfect recipe for what to do with this vision, we have conviction and a clear set of principles.

**RRB** I was fortunate enough to grow up in these neighborhoods. This gave me the chance to see how the street was the best place in which to play and make friends, permanently shaping my idea about the street as a place of exchange, growth, and tight-knit social relations. The city is no more and no less than an urban system of reintegration. Street life makes better citizens; streets are spaces where we are all exactly equal and where we can develop values impossible to acquire anywhere else.

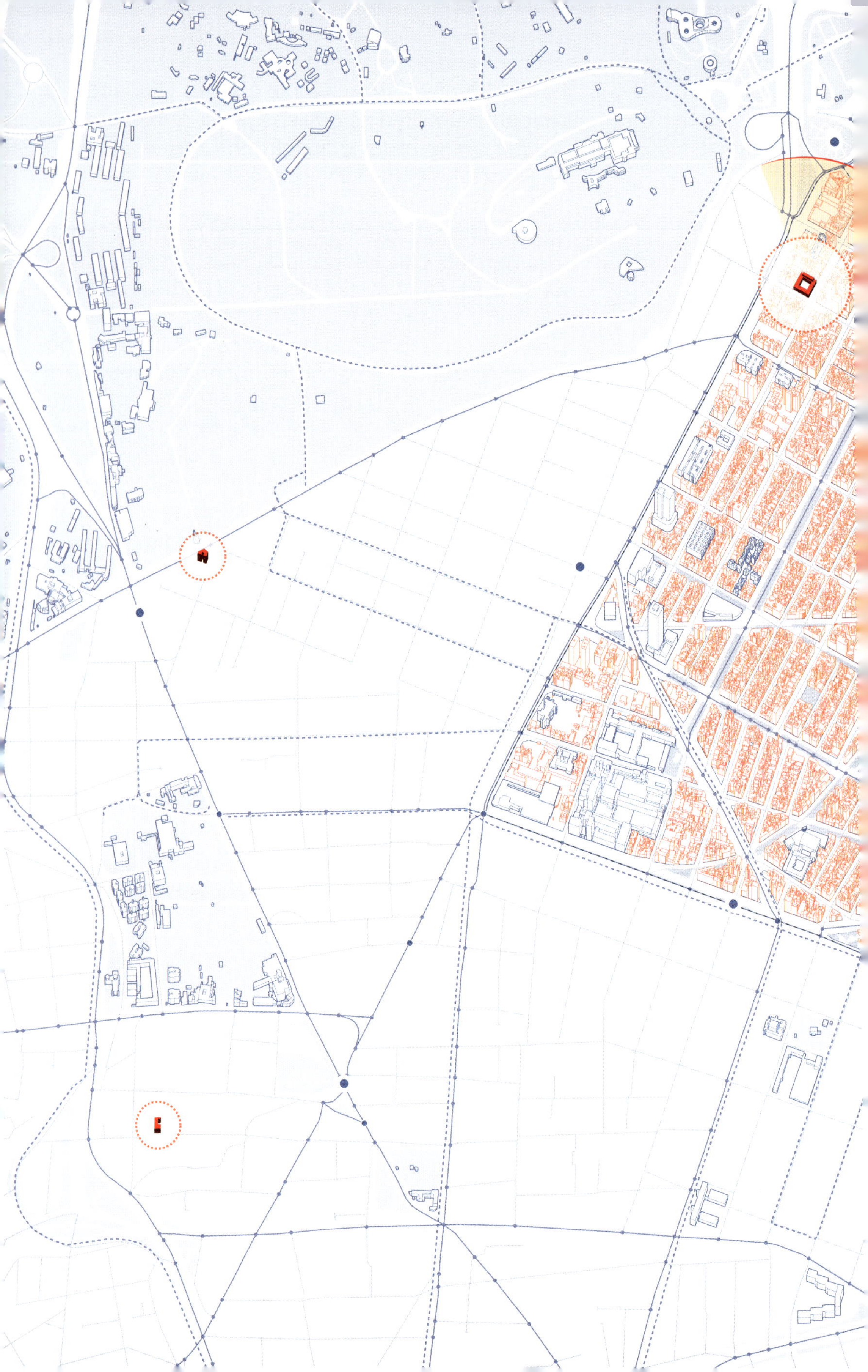

Neighborhood boundaries
Radius of influence
ReUrbano projects
Urban equipment and heritage
Neighborhood buildings
Green areas
Streets
Main avenues
Metrobús stations
Metro stations
Cycle lanes
0
300

Aprende a Cantar
55 44 52 24 34
TAROT

AVENIDA AMSTERDAM

EDIFICIO TERESA
288

124

MEZCALERIA
ANTOLINA

EDIFICIO

**AK** In ten years from now, I think we'd like to see us changing the city, changing it for the better. It's about taking the philosophy further, and by adding different projects we can invest in improving the streets, which is a space for everyone. I think real-estate developments are ideally placed to benefit citizens by integrating public spaces. They can also provide the same service through cultural and education initiatives and other aspects of real-estate developments because, although we focus on housing, we realize that other activities make the largest impact. Going back to the laboratory concept, a part of each project can involve painting part of a street for children to play on Milán street, because whoever uses it will become my neighbor and through this small gesture I'll be helping to build a community. This makes us happy to know that we are helping to sow seeds, even through small projects: like that fruit-seller who is now going to open another stall, demonstrating the same philosophy of maximizing the impact on the city.

Neighborhood boundaries
Radius of influence
ReUrbano projects
Urban equipment and heritage
Neighborhood buildings
Green areas
Streets
Main avenues
Metrobús stations
Metro stations
Cycle lanes

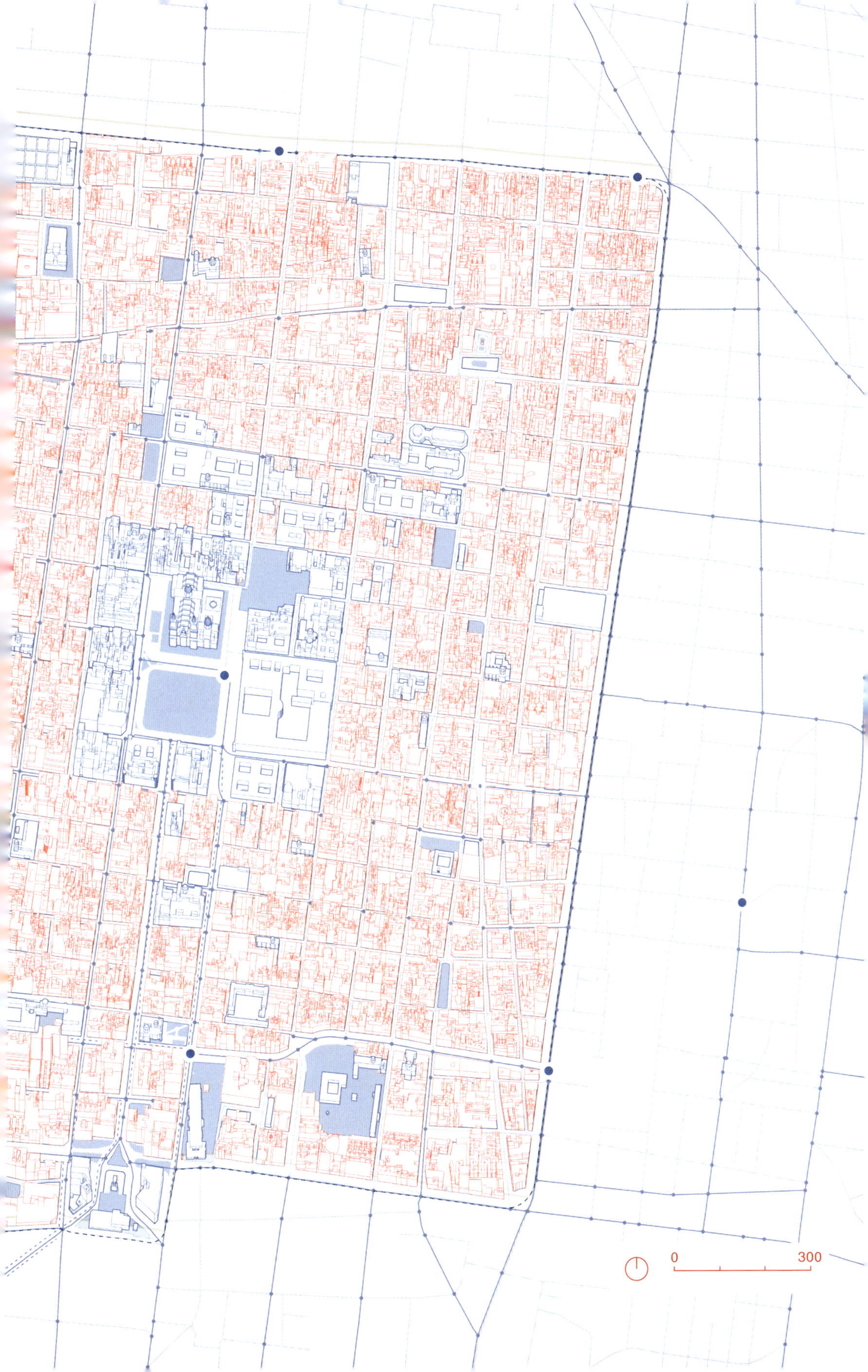
0
300

CDMX

IPN

simon
simon

MAGIA
MAQUILLAJE PROFESIONAL
BROMAS
BROMAS
MAGO

ATENAS
MILENIO

ZARA

EDIFICIO
HEROES
1940

**RRB** The philosophy that we mentioned involves thinking about and focusing on users. We have received many awards for our built work, but ultimately these overlook the real story about their wider impact, one that was truly valuable. Our obligation is to build and design well, but this reveals nothing about what happens between people and users who work in the surrounding areas. We need to fix our attention on this kind of benefit for a proper evaluation of projects. This is why I think we are shifting away from the private and toward the public space, because we can make more of an impact in the public sphere. And also we're moving away from objects and toward users, because although it's good to think about architecture, architecture has to respond to the user. This requires us to think about the unbuilt space, the void. A street of 60 residents is the ideal place for an intervention. Instead of making an impact on the house, you can act at the street level and improve the life of 60 people. Finally, we have to stop talking about single projects and instead think about series of projects. This makes you approach your work more responsibly, not as a unit but as interconnected projects that recognize reciprocal influences. I like to imagine a ReUrbano that enables us to participate in a dynamic of long-term investment and value creation for more people, more fairly and more evenly distributed.

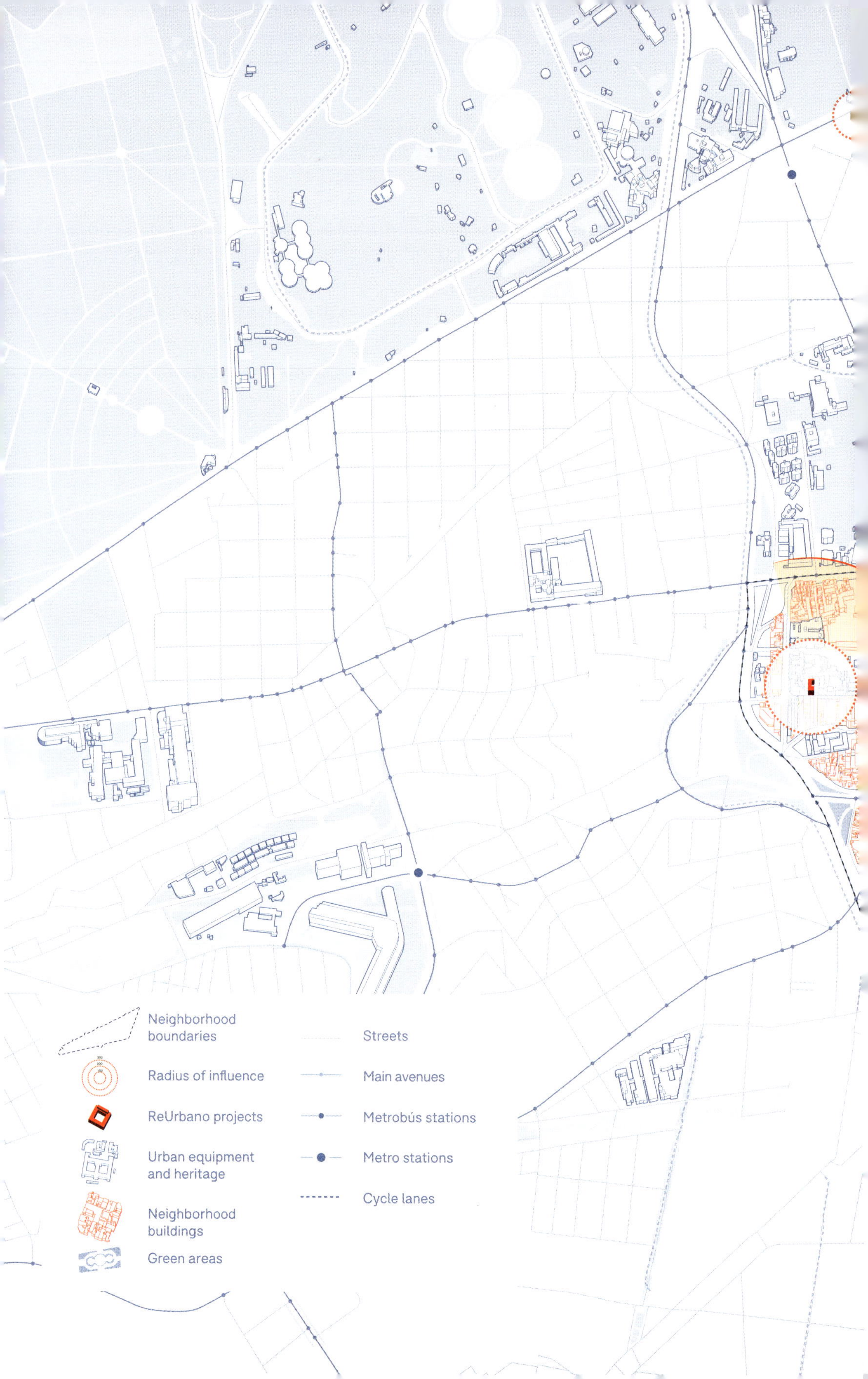
Neighborhood boundaries
Radius of influence
ReUrbano projects
Urban equipment and heritage
Neighborhood buildings
Green areas
Streets
Main avenues
Metrobús stations
Metro stations
Cycle lanes

0
300

TACUBAYA
REPARACION
DE
CALZADO

TACUBAYA
BAÑOS TACUBAYA
BANOS

MERCADO
EL CHORRITO

GNP
24

**AK** If we could give one piece of advice to a future developer, I think we would emphasize the importance of being patient and not sacrificing convictions and ideas, at the same time as being pragmatic and negotiating to achieve agreements and to lose fear of involving others. In our case we began thinking that everything was about private initiative, but we soon realized that we had to bring others on board. Cities are not run by developers but by citizens committed to their professions, to each other, and to their local environment.

**RRB** Partnerships are essential, but they require trust and co-responsibility. If you manage to secure a partnership, projects will endure, be less aggressive and become stronger, attracting support for more complex decisions.

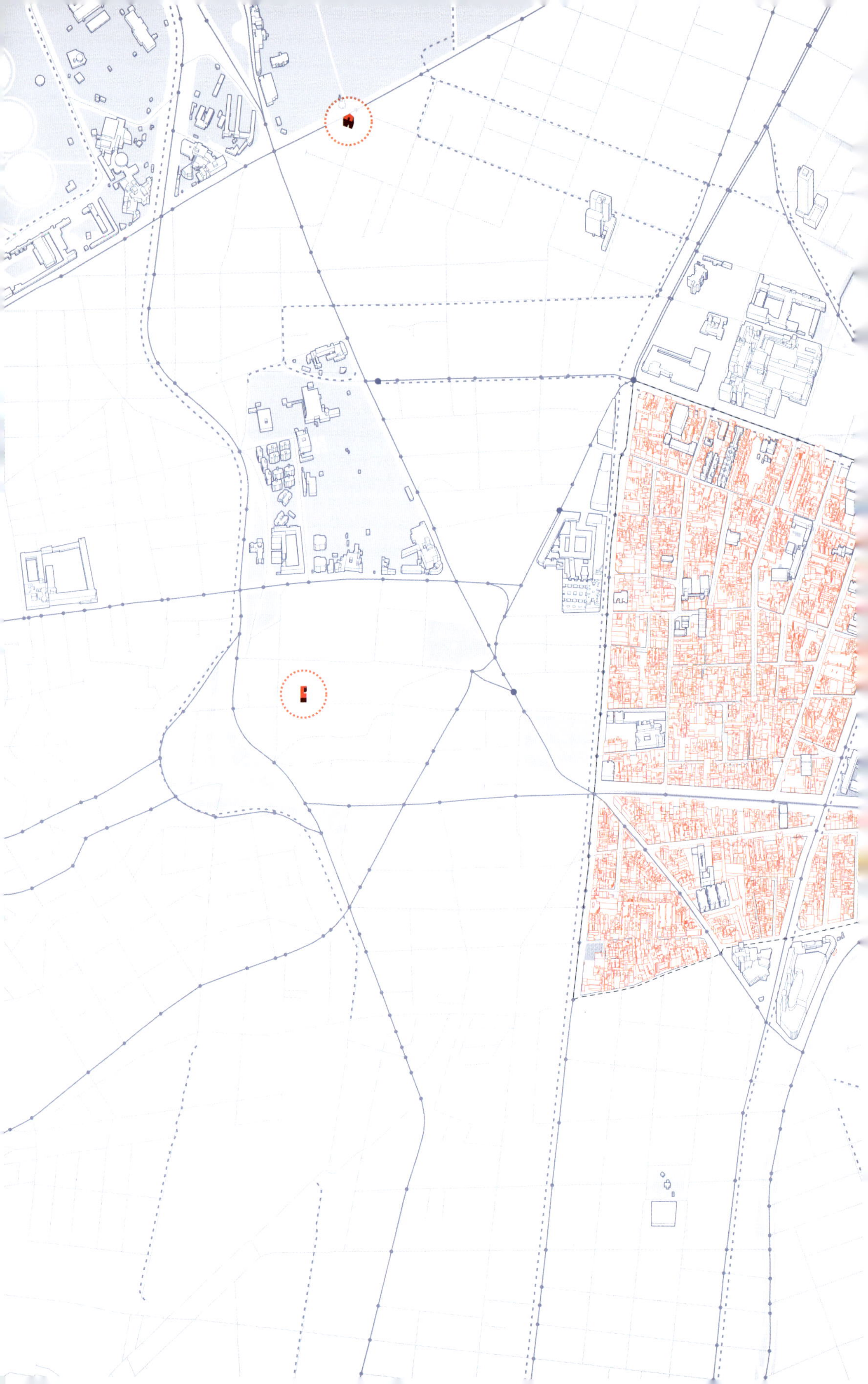

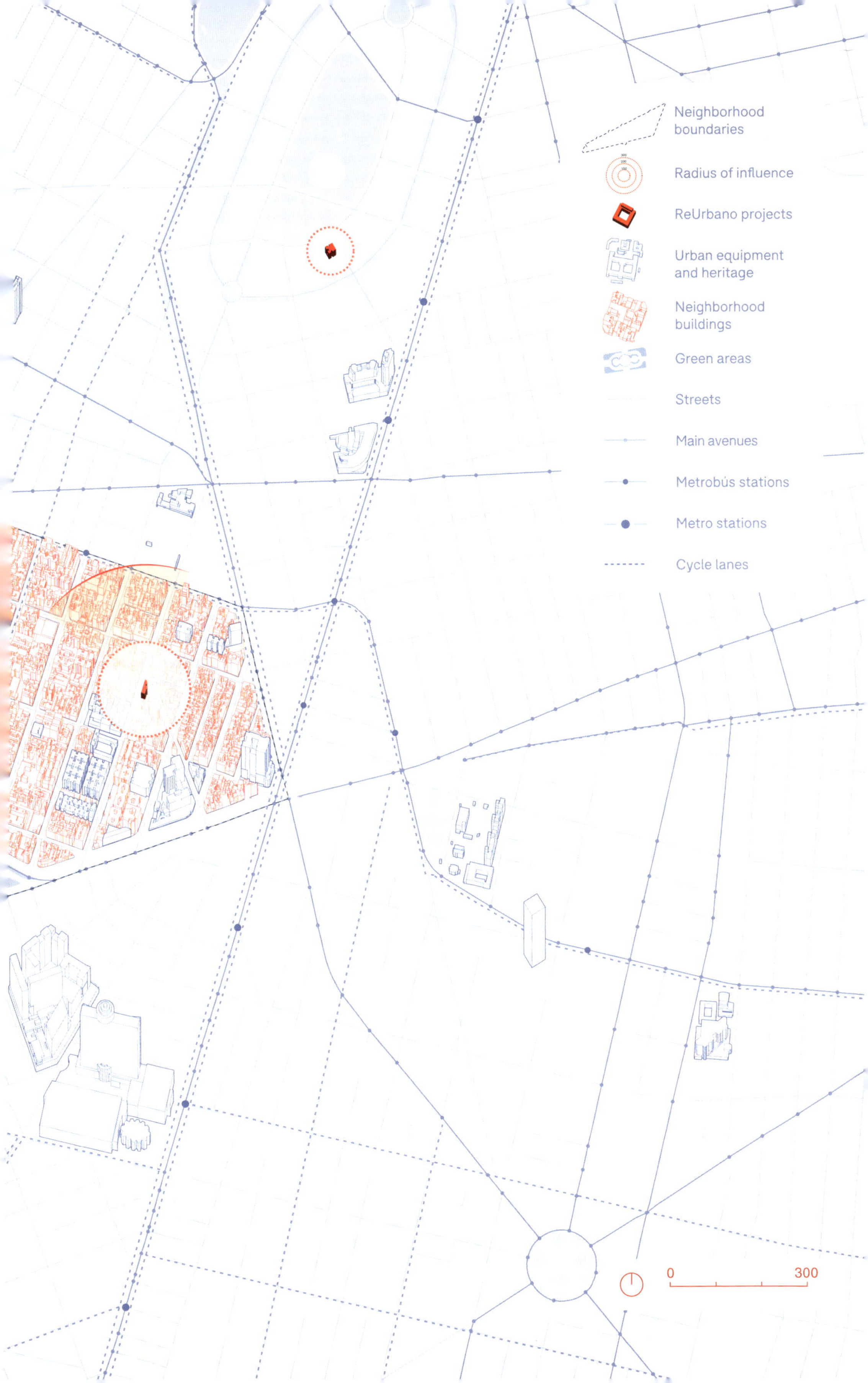
Neighborhood boundaries
Radius of influence
ReUrbano projects
Urban equipment and heritage
Neighborhood buildings
Green areas
Streets
Main avenues
Metrobús stations
Metro stations
Cycle lanes
0
300

La Michoacana
PALETERIA Y NEVERIA
MICHOACANA

la chula
taquería

TINTORERIA
PROGRESO

BIENVENIDOS
CAMBIO DE ACEITE
FRENOS Y CLUTCH
HOJALATERIA Y PINTURA

TALLER de
REPARACION
SOMBRERERIA
ESCANDON

EL LEON DE ORO
LEON
DE ORO
CANTINA
CABRITO

**AK** Following our convictions, I imagine the city in 100 years time and I envisage Mexico City as an urban environment with a good location and unique microclimate to continue growing with greater density, more openness, and in a friendlier way. At ReUrbano we would like to play a central role in this process, and we will have to move beyond building physical spaces in which to live and inhabit. We need to think about virtual spaces and texts to dialog and tell urban stories about the projects created according to this model of city with their virtues. The time has come to open the laboratory and show others what has been gestating, open to questions and criticisms, as we continue reflecting on and adapting our work, helping to build a better city.

Neighborhood boundaries
Radius of influence
ReUrbano projects
Urban equipment and heritage
Neighborhood buildings
Green areas
Streets
Main avenues
Metrobús stations
Metro stations
Cycle lanes

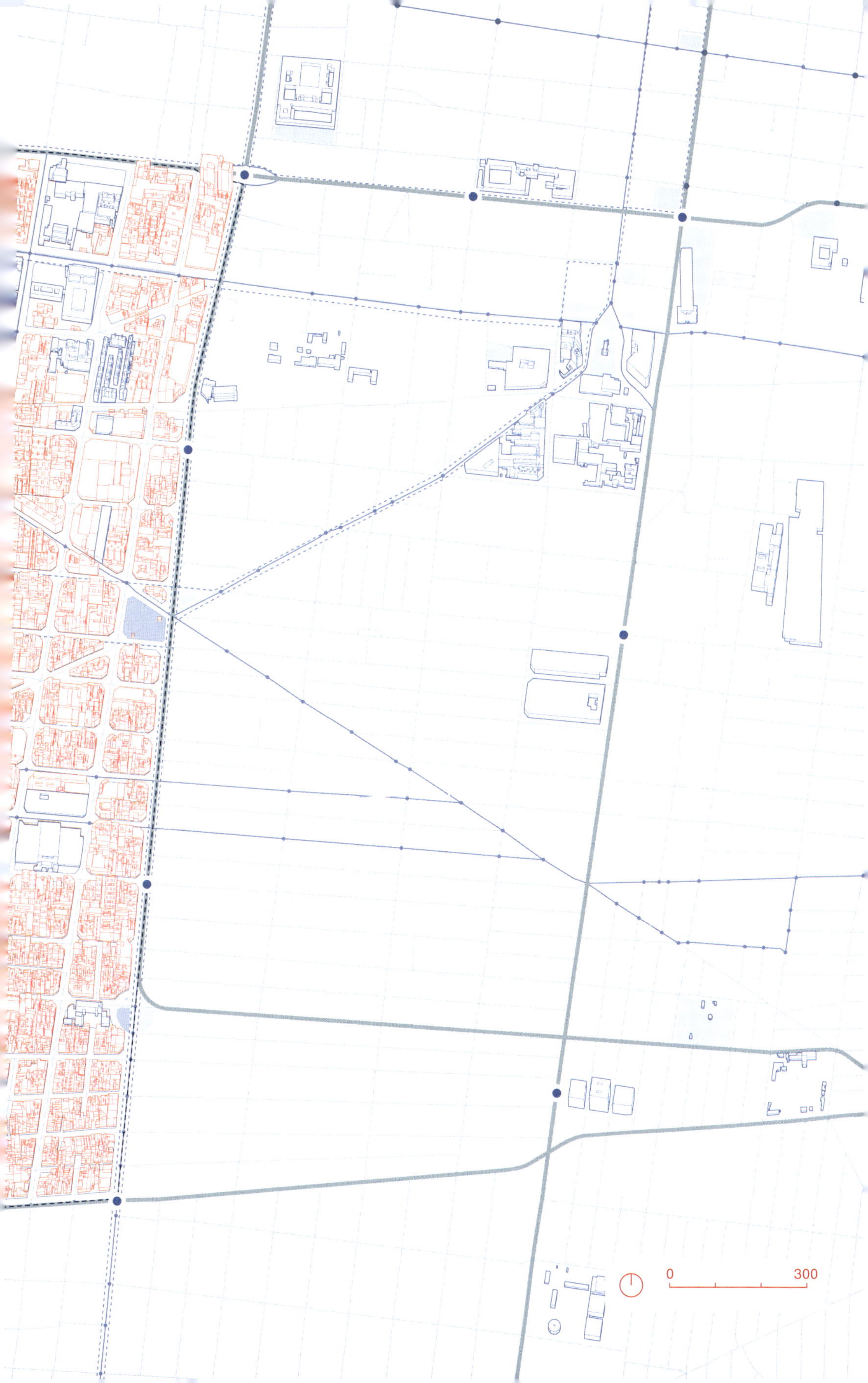
0
300

DO BRASIL
SERVICIO DE CAFETERIA
Americano

AVALÚOS

GRACIAS POR NO ESTACIONARSE
181

LIGA

# Processes

Conservation and Resistance

Consciously Shared Space

Confronting Regulations

The Value of Design

What comprises a city's heritage?

What is our role with existing heritage? What do we keep and what do we change?

Who participates in building a city's heritage, and how?

How do we redefine our heritage under shifting economic, social, and environmental conditions?

What is the city that we want and what are its characteristics?

How do we direct urban developments toward empowering the community?

What kind of participative design strategies should be implemented?

How do we make sure we respond to collective needs in the built environment?

How can we disseminate and question regulations in a productive way?

Where is the value in democratizing such processes and information?

How do we make regulations more relevant to citizens for the common good?

What media and type of citizen participation do we need?

---

In which areas does design have an impact on the urban environment?

How do we go about designing public and private spaces, and especially in the borders and transitions?

What kind of neighborhoods, communities, and cities are created by different design processes?

Who should take part in urban and architectural design processes to build a better city?

# Conservation and Resistance

Projects Without Parking Spaces: A Window Onto Heritage

Urban Recycling: Preserving What Already Exists

Resignifying the Past: Present-Future Interventions

Re-Habilitating: Continuous Successions

Properties In Use: Memory is Not Static

Democratizing Space: City-Making Together

Connecting Urban and Social Issues: Local Memories

# Conservation and Resistance

## Gabriela Etchegaray

Heritage—or what ReUrbano considers heritage—is one of the most valuable starting points for urban renewal.

For ReUrbano, heritage is not only what is worth preserving on account of its structural or artistic merit, but also what is constructed over time from citizens' perspective. The concept of heritage emerged in the 17th century along with a new social awareness capable of recognizing the heritage value of older buildings and architecture. However, as a legacy of the past, we must preserve heritage, as it can easily vanish—it can be destroyed, demolished, or devalued, sometimes even erasing the untold stories of entire communities.

Memory and architectural heritage are inseparable because space is always an aide-memoire. In short, memory is the glue that binds together any society that has evolved over the years. A society that considers architecture as a mere object will be forgotten, because architecture is also a space for its inhabitants' collective memories.

> **ReUrbano preserves and gives new meanings to the properties it develops, and to their neighborhoods and corresponding programs.**

Architecture, as a possible heritage object, has historically had a dual role that combines politics and memory. In fact, we only need to look around us now to realize that in any revolution, the first thing that happens is the destruction of architecture that stores memories. The explanation is simple: demolishing architecture means destroying memories, and destroying memories erodes the identity of a community.

Aloïs Riegl, historian and author of the *Modern Cult of Monuments*, defends the instrumental value of architecture and heritage. Riegl believes in monuments' ability to adapt to new lifestyles and provide containers for 21st-century lives. In line with Riegl's argument, for heritage to be effective in future years, it must not be considered as something static or as a relic; instead, a well-conserved remnant of the past can modify the recollections of those living around it and on a broader scale, the memory of society as a whole.

Heritage can leverage the future, or provide the foundations for further construction. It is not created by objects of absolute value—things that are valuable outside their context—but by objects whose use has made them valuable. Therefore, cultural heritage is dynamic, open, and permanently at the mercy of new additions that citizens can perceive, architects can value, and developers can protect. This happens when ReUrbano decides to preserve—at whatever the cost—certain properties previously considered valueless, in order to revive them. By adopting these strategies, ReUrbano reveals the still-hidden value of certain spaces of the past, constructions that had been left by the wayside. And if we limit ourselves to conceiving heritage as a closed inventory of places covered by the patina of longevity, it will be difficult to

> **To construct a city with memory begins by understanding the importance of heritage.**

expand this catalogue in the future or to defend the inclusion and protection of new properties worth remembering.

**To preserve the heritage is not merely about leaving façades intact, but rescuing complete structures to reoccupy them with new uses that reflect contemporary lifestyles.**

The desire to protect heritage is about avoiding oblivion. ReUrbano works closely with architects, recognizing architecture as a field that creates the right conditions for city-making—conditions that help a society build its memory, context, and relations. For ReUrbano, heritage relates to that city-making process. And preserving it is not about keeping façades intact but rescuing complete structures to reoccupy them and reinhabit them with new uses that do not efface their past.

The complex analysis to detect what should or should not be preserved in urban settings requires a cross-disciplinary approach, ranging from restoration to anthropology and sociology. It also requires collaboration between everyone working on a particular project: clients, developers, architects, local authorities, neighbors. An alliance becomes essential in order to detect potentially valuable heritage. And entering into dialogue with the past is no longer a privilege and instead becomes a need, because the defense and reuse of the city's heritage can bring communities together, and also because reprogramming heritage assets is a defense against rapid and relentless urban transformations. Only by building memories can we slow the universality of contemporary architecture, which transmutes cities until they become generic. And if heritage is to go beyond the listed buildings in an institutional catalogue, then everything that helps build up the collective memory can help avoid the typically banal architecture produced by real-estate developers.

**And if heritage is to go beyond the listed buildings in an institutional catalogue, then everything that helps build up the collective memory can help avoid the typically banal architecture produced by real-estate developers.**

# Projects Without Parking Spaces: A Window Onto Heritage

It's logical: a city that invests in road infrastructure (beltways, overpasses, and elevated highways) is encouraging car use. Residential buildings with parking spaces not only give incentives to residents owning and depending on cars; they also interrupt the flow on sidewalks, because we end up having to give way to cars constantly going in or out.

*So what happens to stores on the street?*

*And what about people who enjoy walking on the sidewalk without facing constant obstacles and interruptions?*

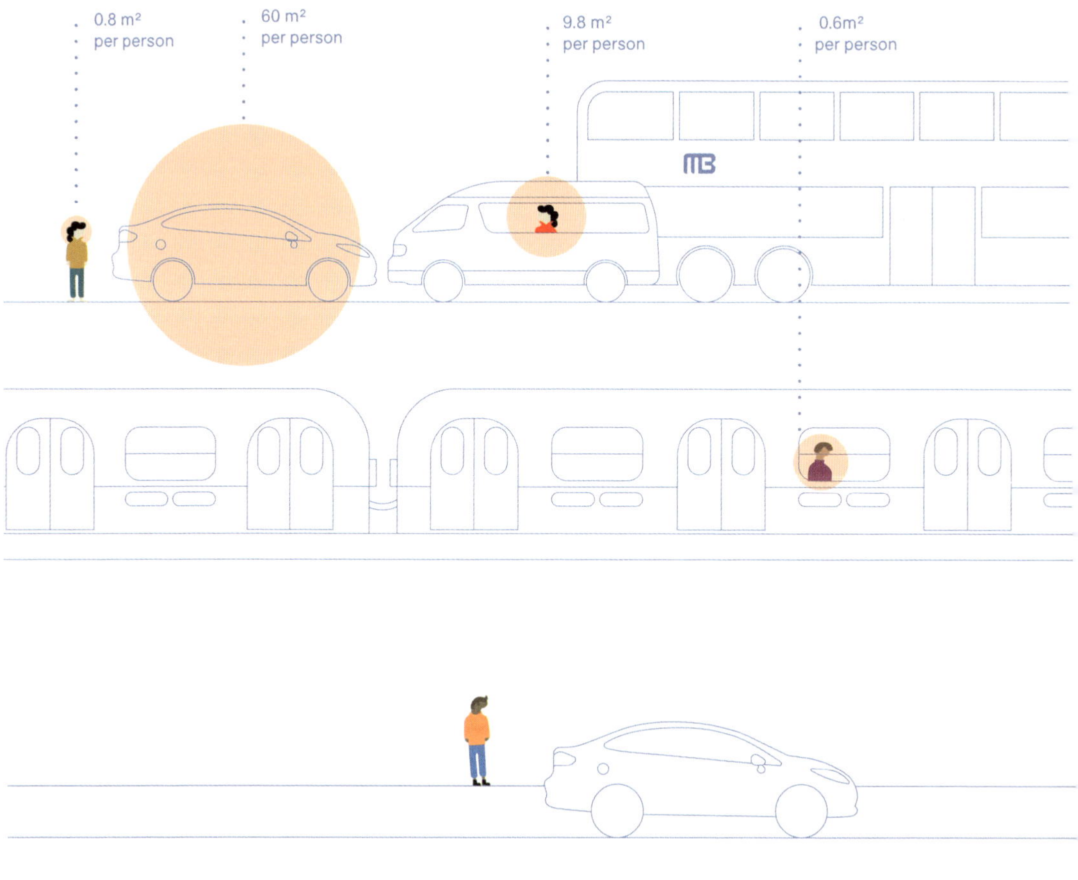

When we discovered in 2010 that more than 40 percent of built space within Mexico City's buildings was reserved for parking spaces, the figure struck us as alarming and illogical. In the city, only 18 percent of the population uses a car to get around. This raises the question: for whom are all the many roads, thoroughfares, and beltways being built?

This marks the beginning of ReUrbano's history. At that point, regulations required residential projects to include at least one parking space for every 120 square meters of floor area, and businesses one for every 40 square meters. To challenge that regulation, firstly of all we had to prove to the authorities and investors that things could be different, that it was possible to develop successful

**What would our community life be like if public transport could be so practical and comfortable that using a car would be the exception rather than the rule?**

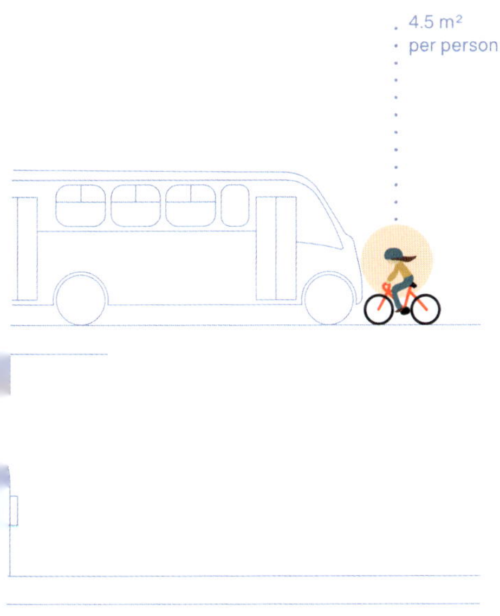


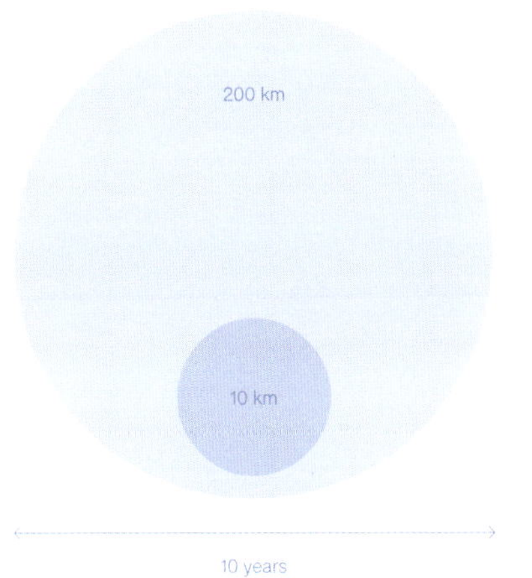

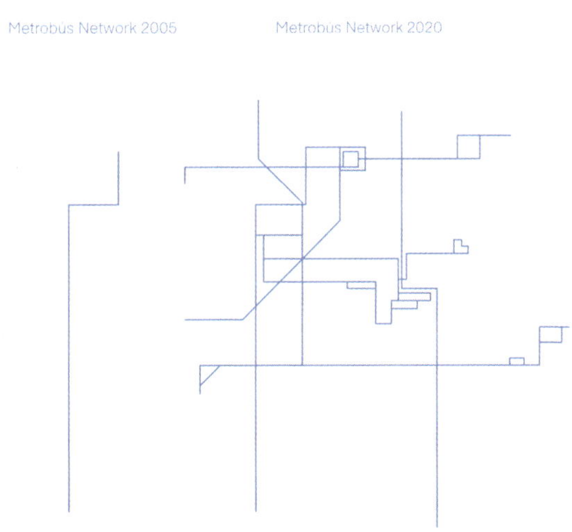

and attractive projects that did not revolve around parking.

We began working with listed buildings because that was where we found the exception to the rule; we could develop housing in them without the requirement to offer the parking spaces required by the regulations. Taking advantage of this exception, we began working on our first projects that legally offered new apartments for sale without parking spaces because we were preserving heritage properties.

Building a city with fewer cars entails the requirement for more investments in public transport. There is also a need to demonstrate that another reality is viable, and even preferable. Prioritizing pedestrians is not something whimsical: studies show that cities which promote pedestrianization of their avenues and alternative transport options are safer and offer a higher quality of life. When we talk about "city-making," our idea is to return pedestrians and citizens to the heart of urban life.

**From an environmental perspective and in the long term, how sustainable is it to continue investing in facilitating the use of cars?**

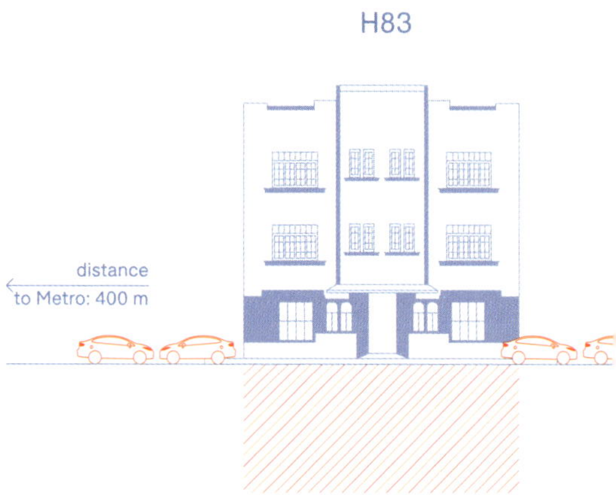


**In cities like Paris, any new building less than 500 meters from the metro does not need to offer parking spaces.**

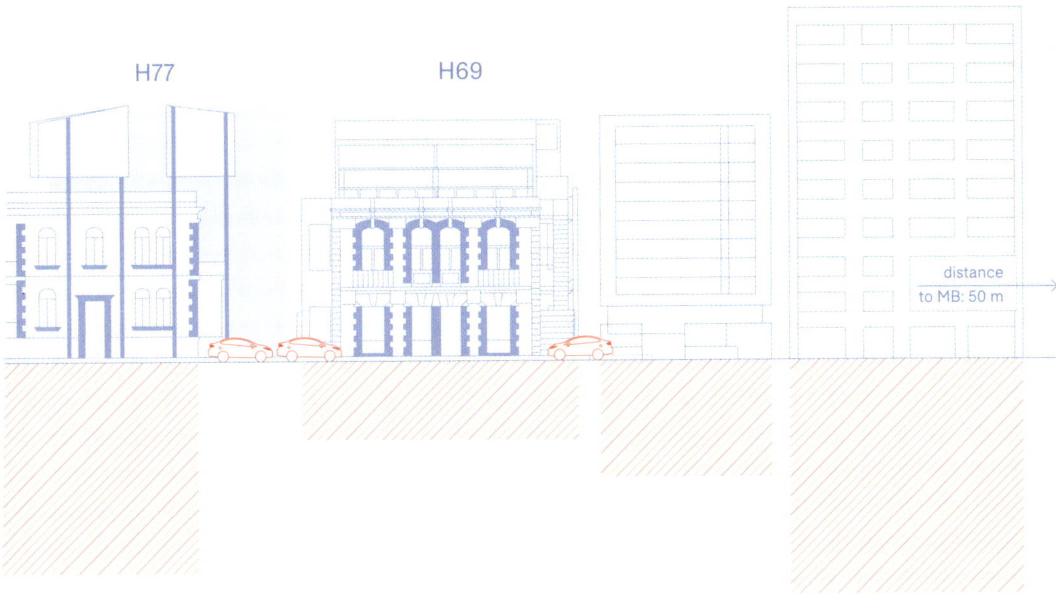


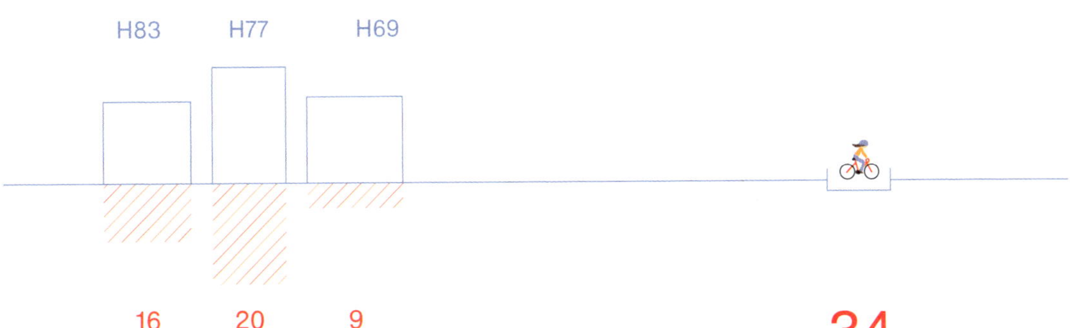


45 parking spaces required

0% built

34
bike parking spaces built
in Havre since 2010

# Urban Recycling: Preserving What Already Exists

What we value in built heritage goes beyond the purely aesthetic. What kind of life does a building promote? What is its impact on residents, neighbors, and society? In a city with such a long and rich history, urban life itself is heritage, and it is worth safeguarding buildings' uses as much as the structures themselves.

Preservation is an act of respecting memory, culture and our history. For ReUrbano, it is not about freezing something in time or creating untouchable objects. The city is a being that breathes and transforms together with the culture it contains. We change it, but it also changes us.

When we see an abandoned, derelict, and therefore vulnerable building, we try to turn things around. This does not mean going back in time but taking what already exists and finding its place in the contemporary world. Our approach to reactivation is not about reviving the glory days of a building or offering glimpses of its past life. We want it to contribute again to urban life as directly as possible.

We also ask ourselves how to determine buildings worth preserving. Some institutions focus on identifying "heritage" but in our experience safeguarding built objects is not only worthwhile for constructions of historical value.

> **The Milán 44 building, for example, was a disused workshop, but its skeleton offered potential as a building open to the street and connected to its surroundings. We extended the life of a building that was valueless in the perception of governmental heritage institutions.**

Auto
Electrica
SSO SA
PARTES ELECTRICAS PARA:

Auto
Electrica
Casso
ACCESORIOS
AUTO ELECTRICA CASSO, S.A. DE C.V.
PARTES ELECTRICAS PARA:
44

BARRIO·ABARROTES·COMIDA

# Resignifying the Past: Present-Future Interventions

How do we approach resignifying a building's vocation? By acknowledging the past and understanding present conditions to harmonize them.

Located in the Doctores neighborhood, the 1920s Laguna building was formerly a textile factory before eventually becoming derelict. In 2018, we renovated the construction, creating a space for a new generation of designers and manufacturers of ceramic and wooden items. One can still feel a sense of craftmanship within its walls.

The city, like the society to which it belongs, is not unchanging: it changes over time, exchanging one set of needs for another. This project shows our interest in connecting past and present, preserving the vocation for craftmanship and looking ahead to a future capable of connecting complex and diverse relationships between the old and the new, the local and the national.

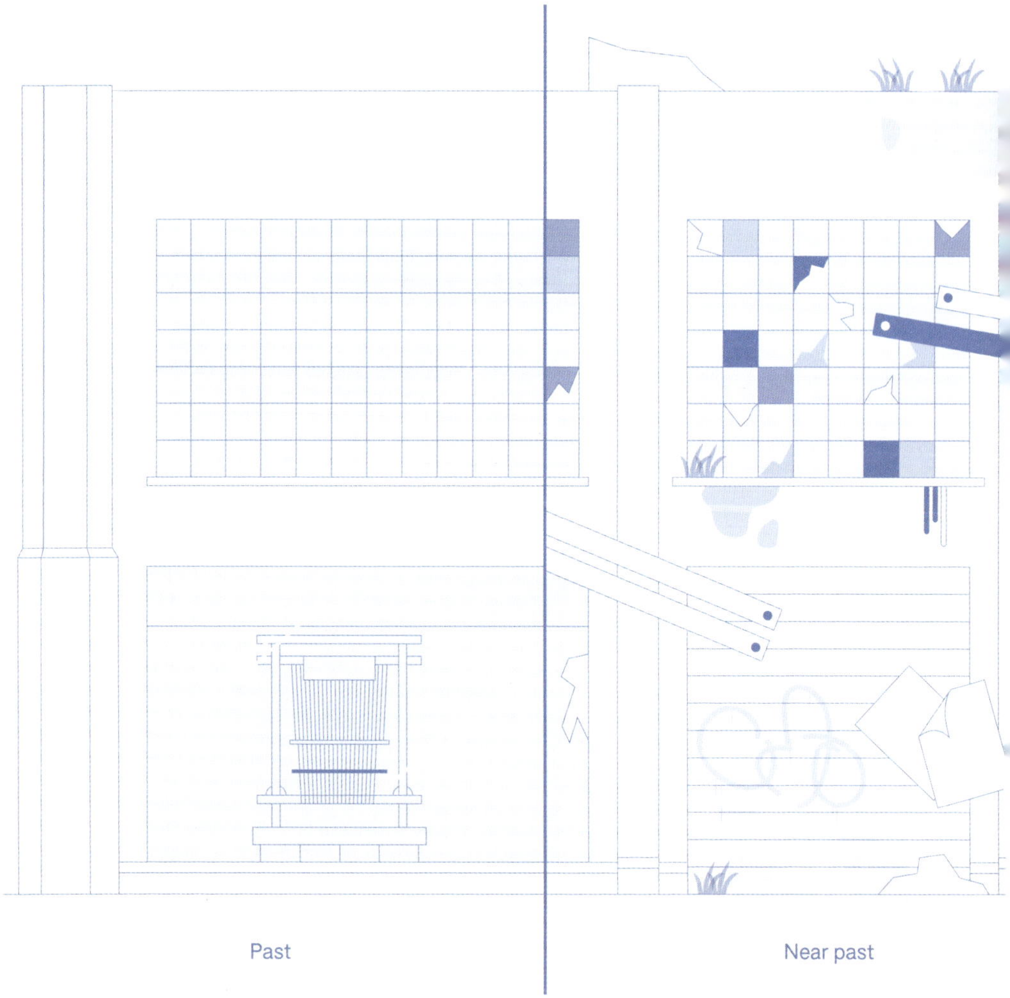

Past

Near past

Present

# Re-Habilitating: Continuous Successions

Every abandoned property has its own history. When we start conceiving ways to reactivate it, our first task is to ask ourselves what was there before. What happened within these walls? What was the building's relation to the city? The meticulous preservation process can take anything from a few months up to a couple of years, and this period offers an opportunity to explore and expand ways of inhabiting it. In the interval between a building's abandonment and its new life a moment exists when its function is ambiguous, amorphous and ideal for ephemeral projects.

Before acquiring a permanent use, our projects have provided a venue for fairs, bazaars, art exhibitions, and community events. They have also been the starting point for many neighborhood architectural tours.

This intermediate phase of our projects has enabled us to achieve three things:

- to offer a experimental and exhibition space for various initiatives that benefit the community and culture.
- to create partnerships with neighborhoods' creative communities.
- to explore spatial possibilities and to gain an in-depth understanding of a building's character and qualities.
- to take stock of the abandoned state by inviting the general public to imagine the building's "before" and "after" phase. This involves various people as active participants in our process and restores the building's purpose and raison d'être: to build stories on a daily basis.

We believe in our buildings' life. These temporary and community reactivations reflect our insistence that a building should not be abandoned, left empty and lifeless. It is also a part of our methodology; our process of imagining and pushing the boundaries with a building's potential. We believe that a construction's fluctuating essence depends on the life that users give it at a specific moment and, on a broader scale, on its relationship to its social and built context.

SSO. S.A. DE C.V.
MÓVIL

**We believe that a construction's essence depends on the life that users give it and, on a broader scale, on its relationship to its social and built context.**

# Properties In Use: Memory is Not Static

## How to renovate and preserve a building without treating it as a precious object?

Regulations on architectural heritage usually focus on objects' physical conservation, while architecture is focused on habitation.

Approaching an old building as if it were a museum piece is to rob it of its function and character. Mexico City has a rich history and significant spatial requirements and therefore any renovation project needs to provide new uses.

We believe that heritage properties cannot be static because they preserve collective memories that are transformed together with society, which in turn also transforms over time. When we work on a building, our idea is to respect the structure without this preventing us from starting a new chapter in its history, one that is relevant to its contemporary context and that can reinsert the building into a city that is constantly on the move

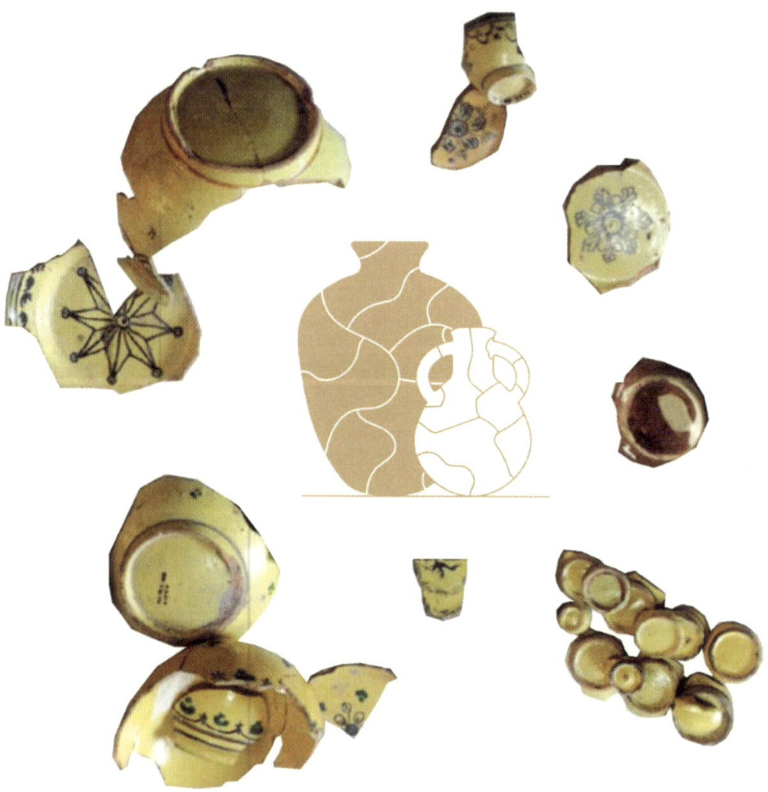

**The national law on heritage buildings makes it possible to explore Mexico City through the permits granted for projects involving listed buildings; we can draw a map of pre-Hispanic and colonial settlements outside the very center of the city. Márquez Sterling 28 A is an early-20th-century building where we discovered a vast number of old pieces of ceramic. In total, the study analyzed 2,991 pots, 58 of which belong to the pre-Hispanic era and 2,879 to the city's colonial period.**

# Democratizing Space: City-Making Together

Working to create an ideal city involves interpreting, managing, moderating, communicating, and bringing together participants from the public and private sectors. In that sense, ReUrbano's projects require far more than drawing, building, and selling.

In each of our projects, the process consists of gathering a team of architects, builders, investors, government officials, and neighbors. Our business model requires us to adhere to market regulations and conditions. This leads us to ask: How can we develop properties that are both profitable and have a positive social impact?

Throughout our careers we have constantly found that we will not arrive at an answer on our own, perhaps because there is no single response.

## Cities that benefit everyone need to be built collaboratively.

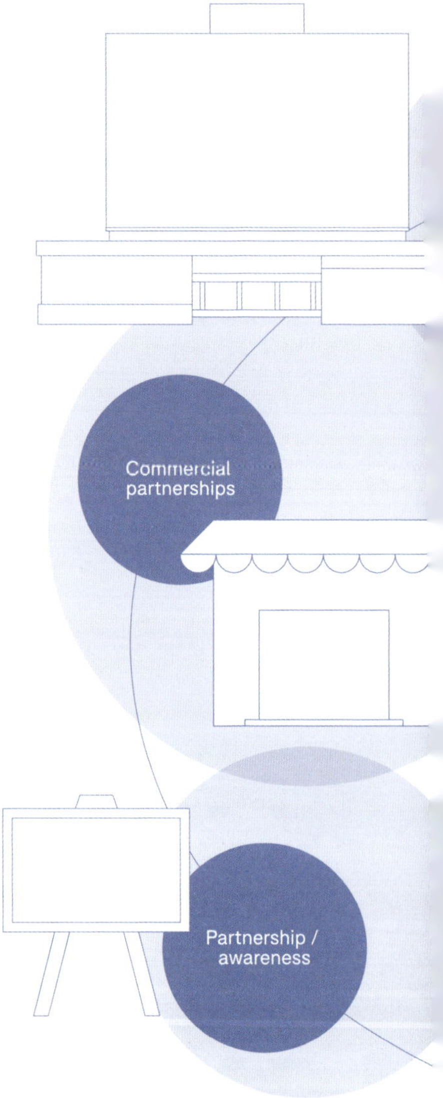

International architects, urbanism, restoration
Collaborations
Institutions
Investors
Financial institutions / investors
Publications and references

# Connecting Urban and Social Issues: Local Memories

*Barrio (noun). Part of a relatively homogenous urban area, with vague boundaries, which forms a basic unit in the perception of urban life. [...] The barrio shows signs of a collective identity as a place where people live and go about their daily lives. [...] Not every individual aspect of the barrio is spatially or socially homogenous.*

*—Diccionario de Urbanismo*

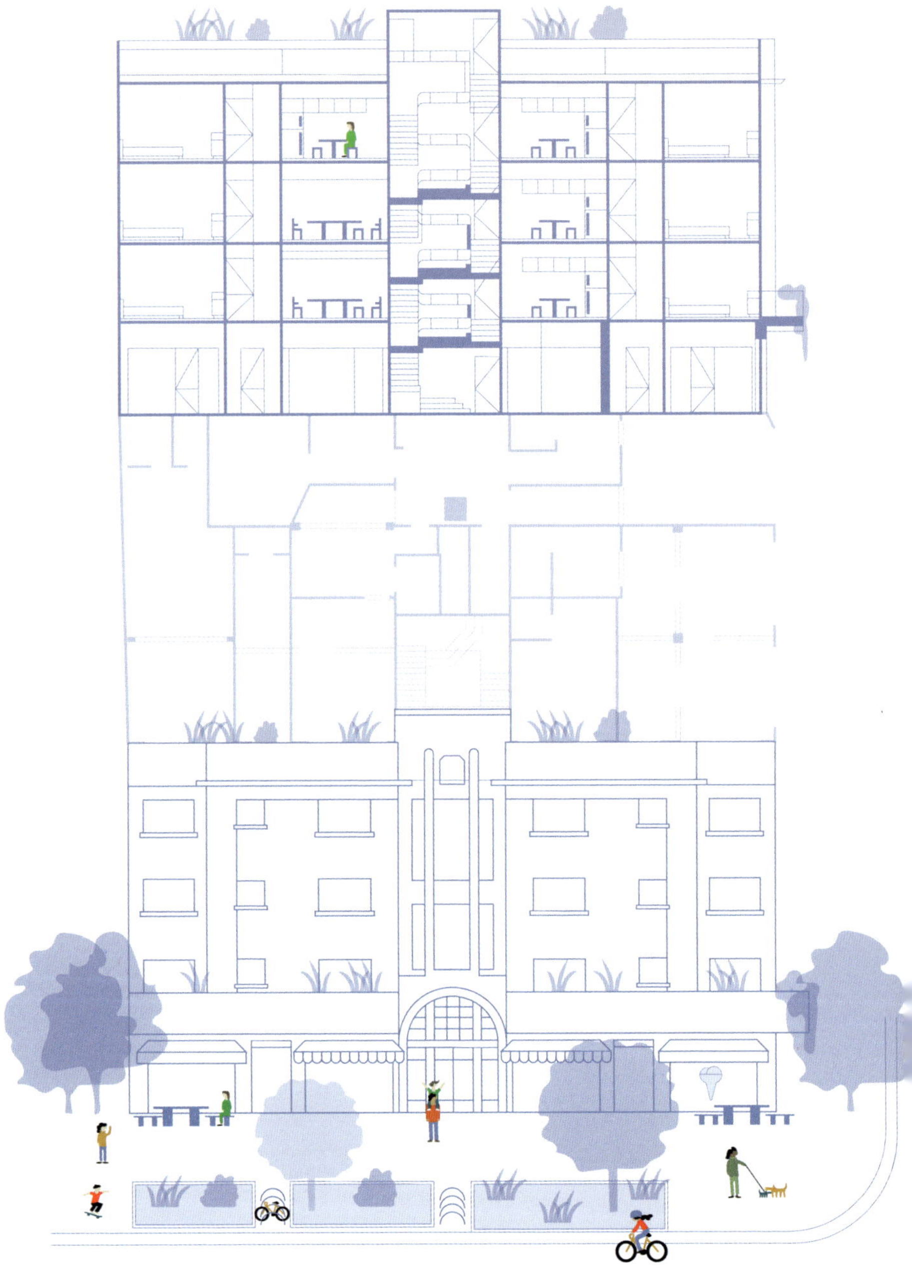

We have shown how, for ReUrbano, the value of Mexico City's central barrios does not lie solely in their historical constructions. The collective memory is infinitely complex and is not built by preserving or replicating the iconic features of some heritage façades.

Every barrio has local businesses founded by members of the community, often passed down through the generations, which give a distinctive identity to the local areas. We cannot talk about being committed to preserving the heritage of these neighborhoods without protecting these businesses, the ones that give each barrio its local flavor and which, taken together, weave together the city's urban and social fabric.

Acknowledging the person behind a desk is something deeply human, in the sense of familiarity that we develop with spaces by frequenting them. What is the community without this? The neighborhoods where we work have all kinds of stores and businesses catering to a wide range of budgets and requirements. The ice-cream parlors, cafés, stationers, and corner stores are also a part of our day-to-day lives. We keep this in mind when asking what kind of businesses we are seeking to promote in our developments.

**An ice-cream parlor called La Michoacana occupied the ground floor of Liverpool 9. When we acquired the building, we had the option to replace it with another business, but we ended up retaining it. Therefore, although we opened a new chapter in the building's history, a part of its essence lives on.**

# Consciously Shared Space

Supporting Local Life: People, Business, and Customs

Community Under Construction: Other Financing Options

Occupying a Place: Lessons Learned for Future Projects

Urban Corridors: A Study of the City and the Unbuilt Environment

A Greater Good: Beyond the Daily Routine

Blurring the Boundaries: Life Outside the Projects

# Consciously Shared Space

## Gabriela Etchegaray

For Aristotle, the city was where human beings could lead a social life, a place for exchanges and relationships not merely for survival but also for our wellbeing, where we could share, trade, help, or receive help in our daily lives. Public spirit, or rather citizens' coexistence, justifies the existence of cities, a view at odds with the reality of the 21st-century metropolis.

To transfer this Aristotelian notion to our days, we would need to reinterpret today's city as a space for living together. A collective life is a life of trade, dialogue, caring, and proximity. Collectivity is unrelated to populism or socialism, but the rejection of individualism and isolation; individualism runs counter not only to the essence of cities, but also their inherent culture since it has been imposed gradually and subtly by external models of coexistence.

> **Within a city, a building's relationship with its surroundings is as important as what it contains because, beyond its walls, "collective life" takes place, a dynamic that can only exist in public space.**

ReUrbano's work focuses on retraining in the use of collective spaces. The outcome becomes visible in the indeterminate spaces created between private properties and the surrounding public space; areas of encounters for everything or nothing, for exchanges and non-exchanges. ReUrbano works both inside and outside, blurring the boundaries between one and the other. Understanding that programs go beyond private property forms part of a vision that assumes that architecture, as Richard Sennett explains, consolidates the city, and if we want that city to recreate a collectivity we must begin by using what is within our reach as citizens and developers conscious of shared spaces.

**Urban development and architecture therefore stimulate the transformation of collective life, and they can also give citizens a voice and support their social conscience.**

These are the actions ReUrbano describes as "programming and personalizing": strategies that go beyond a building's material boundaries and that require decision-making not only in the physical realm but also in abstract and programmatic terms. Such a decision might or might not take the form of an architectural object that helps to program such spaces, but it must form part of urban projects and integrate them into the collective life through daily experiences.

As developers and as citizens, ReUrbano is co-responsible for consciously considering the possible impacts of each of its interventions, focusing on the micro and macro scale, as part of the city-making process and to respond to those utopian questions about the form that our desired city should take. The combination of housing and business premises encourages pedestrianization to activate interactions; in the contemporary city it is still feasible to cede open, shared spaces and ground-floor areas. These are not utopian measures at all. The neighborhoods chosen for ReUrbano's projects arise from the possibility of promoting diverse uses and public spaces. Together, these conditions promote activities 24 hours a day, 7 days a week, and this in turn increases the sense of safety.

**It is not about deciding whether or not to leave open spaces or freely accessible ground floors, but about what happens in these spaces, who uses them, and what kind of flows of consumption they create.**

Consciously designing shared spaces not only avoids political and economic mistakes, but it also helps to transform these sectors by encouraging collective living and the social cohesiveness created as a result.

# Supporting Local Life: People, Business, and Customs

The homogenization of cities is largely the result of chain stores that have conquered every corner of the world. You can now buy the same hamburger or cup of coffee whether you are in Tokyo, Paris, New York, or Mexico City. But a chain store is not the same as a local store. Its owners do not belong to the host community, and its users do not create unique links to the space or become part of the essence that characterizes a specific neighborhood.

We decided to support local businesses, not as something fashionable or contrarian but because we believe in their invaluable contribution to the social fabric. We consider that a local business that builds up a personal relationship with its users is worthwhile. Although a large chain store can always pay more, we decided to embrace the risk of promoting local entrepreneurs who contribute more to our vision of the city. A diverse city requires diverse users and businesses.

eno
Creamos comunidad
NUESTRO CREDO
Compartimos lo que nos gusta.
Servimos el mejor producto disponible.
Cumplimos nuestra palabra.
Somos detallistas.
Somos consistentes.
Somos agradecidos.
Nos encanta nuestro trabajo.
Creemos en la igualdad.
Respetamos el medio ambiente.
Practicamos la responsabilidad social.
Nada nos detiene.

# Community Under Construction: Other Financing Options

The creative community—especially at an embryonic stage-is a vital part of every thriving neighborhood. We value artistic creativity and culture as an investment in the future.

We have found a way of participating by offering young entrepreneurs, designers, and artists the opportunity to occupy our buildings during their various stages of development. This helps encourage the diversity that we are constantly seeking in our projects, and also offers emerging talents or organizations a platform or space in which to work, plan for the future, and expand.

This is not just a way of reviving buildings and broadening their possibilities; it also helps create communities and is often the first step in establishing partnerships that enrich the neighborhood, community, and history.

4
3
2
1
PB

# Occupying a Place: Lessons Learned for Future Projects

To understand the life of a neighborhood and its community, you need to participate fully. We are always talking with stakeholders to develop a deep relationship with the neighborhoods where we work, and we make an effort for this to be about actions instead of empty talk.

Over the past ten years, our team has occupied various buildings that we have developed, moving from one to another as a means of testing prototypes. Living in what we have built has revealed to us how our developments work in practice and, in a broader sense, the idiosyncrasies of the neighborhoods where we have intervened. At daytime and in the night, what are its noises, available means of transport, public spaces, local businesses? Who lives there, how do they interact, what is important to them?

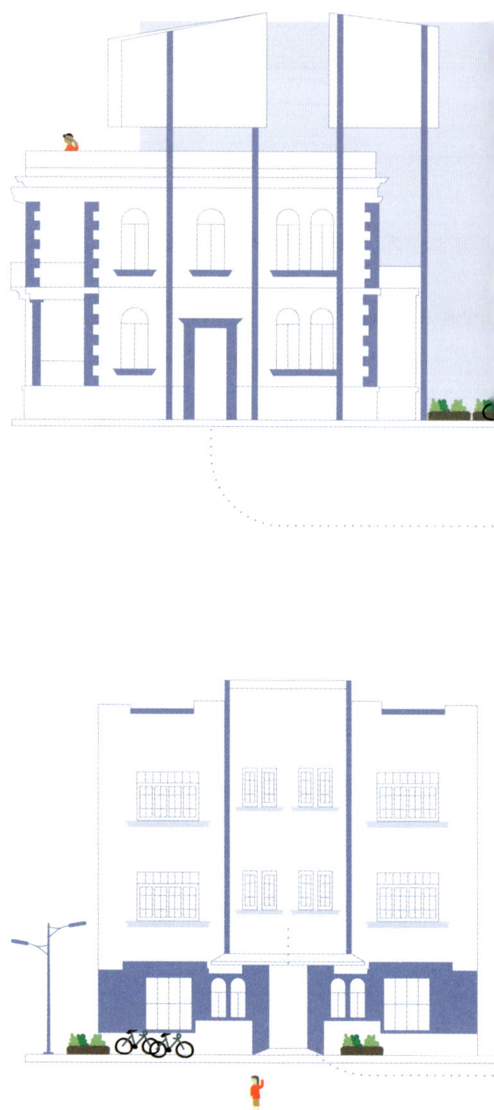

**It's worth asking ourselves how different the city's buildings would be if developers had to be the first people to live in them; what would happen if instead of "listening to the neighbors," they became part of the neighborhoods themselves?**

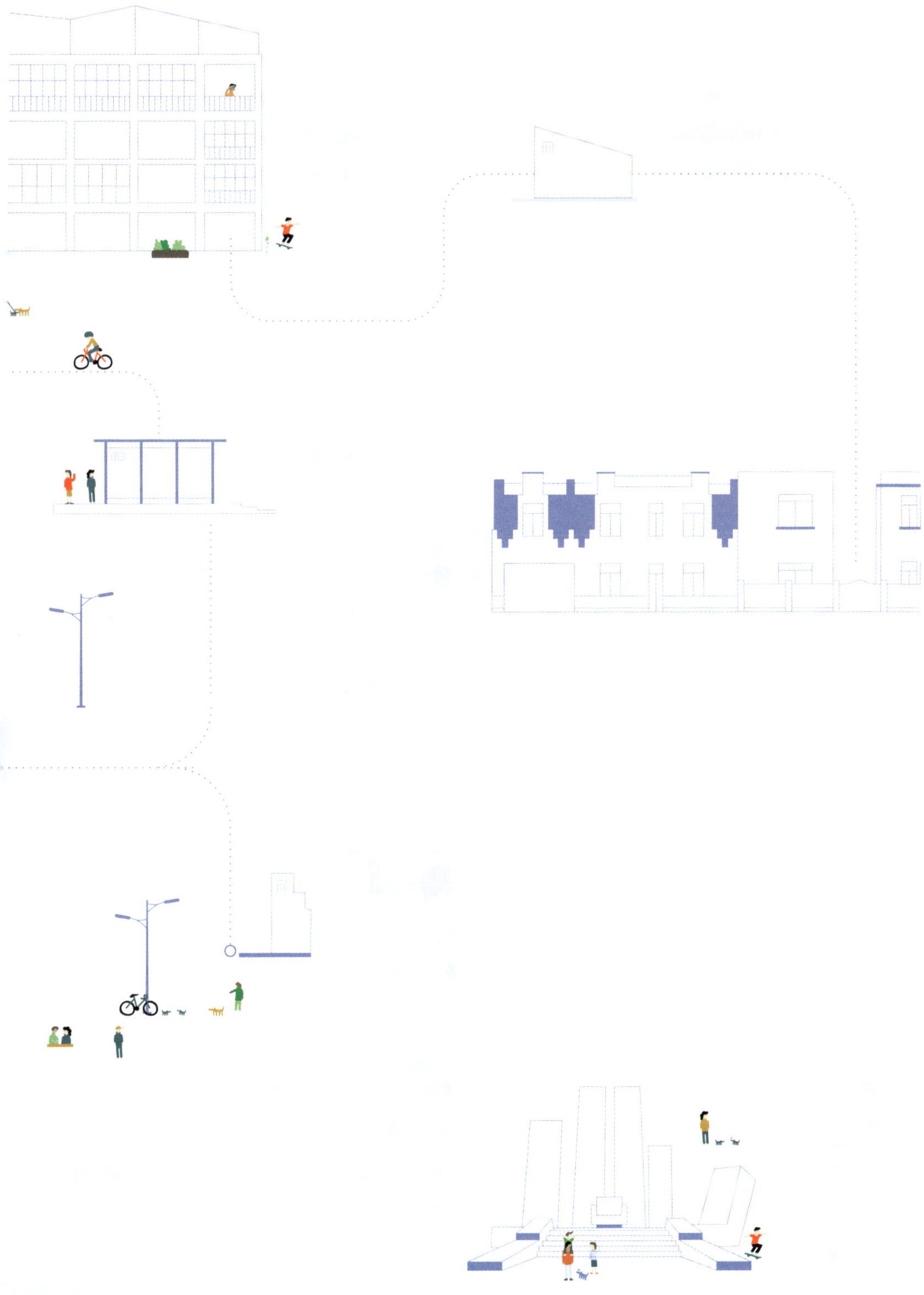

# Urban Corridors: A Study of the City and the Unbuilt Environment

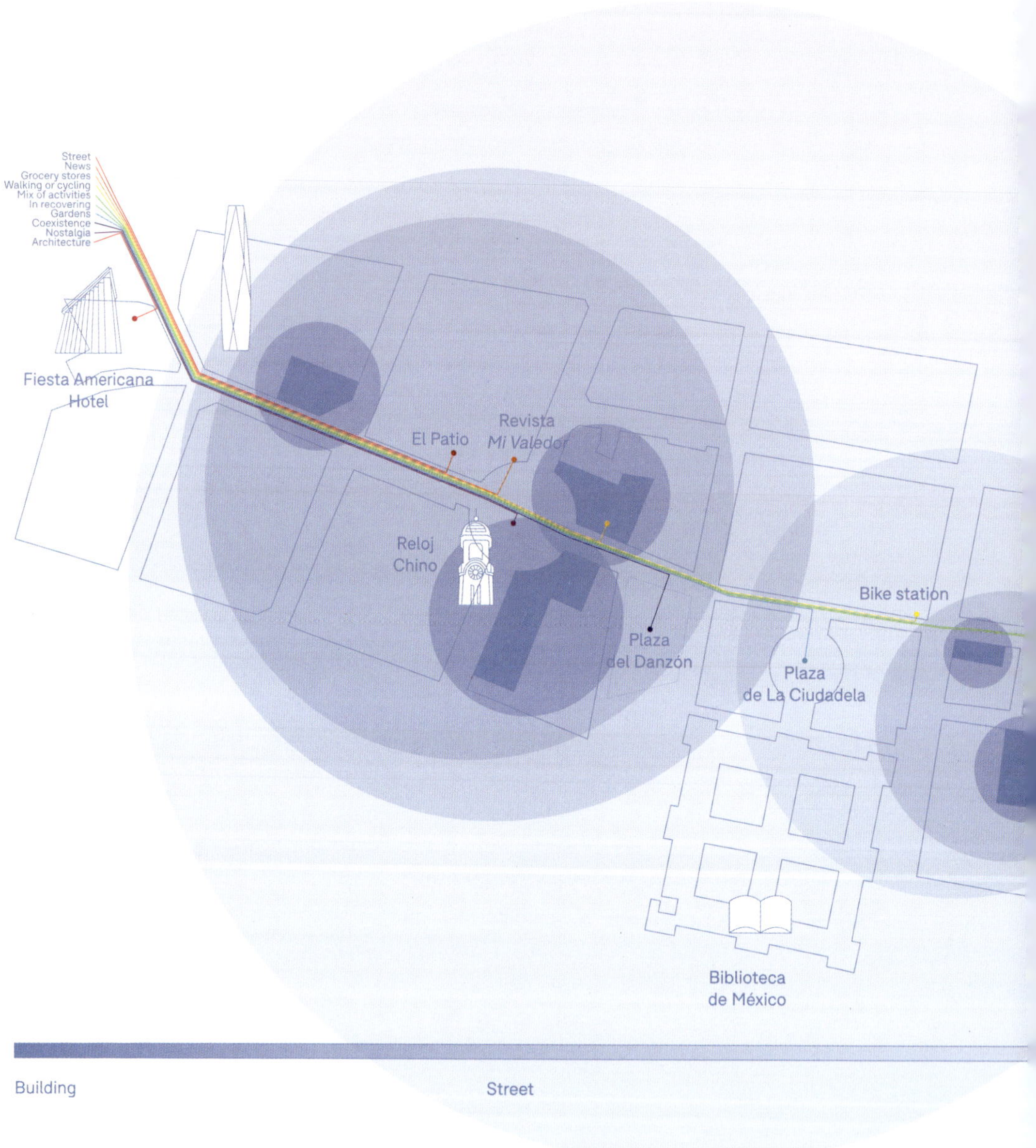

If we begin by asking ourselves what kind of city we want, then the answer will lead us to wondering how to achieve it.

After understanding what happens inside a project and outside it, on the street, we can expand our field of vision to consider an even larger scale. At ReUrbano we talk about "corridors" as a concept that evolves from in-depth studies of the city; from recognizing the place; from the history and people who create the buildings themselves as well as the spaces in-between.

One of our strategies has been to approach projects on a street-by-street, block-by-block basis in order to strengthen relationships between neighbors and to regenerate a part of the city, giving it new uses and inhabitants. We understand the daily use of the city as an added value and we define it as a communal space for people who often have nothing in common.

Plaza Giordano Bruno, Camino a San Juan, and Corredor Hidalgo are all projects sharing the same working model and process, where the first step has been to analyze the area in question. If our projects share values, what will happen in the space separating them if they are close to one another, on a complete corridor? In a broad sense, the idea is that if one active ground floor can give the block a new character, a series of them can generate new dynamics for an entire neighborhood, because the activities on the street will begin to attract neighbors and visitors.

**If one active ground floor can give the block a new character, a series of them can generate new dynamics for an entire neighborhood.**

# A Greater Good: Beyond the Daily Routine

Although ReUrbano's projects form the cor of our work, since the outset we have trie to blur the boundaries, setting ourselves ta gets beyond the regular role of a real-estat developer.

This mentality runs through everythin we do, but it has become particularly urgen and relevant during the moments of crisi endured by our city. The 19 September 201 (19-S) earthquake caused incalculable loss es. When confronted with this crisis, citizen showed levels of solidarity that demonstrat the power of collectivity. As developer neighbors, and with a passion for the city, i was a privilege for us to witness and partic ipate in the resilience of our neighborhoods.

In the immediate aftermath of the earth quake, we realized that we had to play a active role in the recovery efforts and use the resources at our disposal. This explains the origins of the participative project calle "Resiliencia Barrial" (Noighborhod Resilience that had the following objectives:

- To map the citizen initiatives following 19-S, giving visibility to the urban model that emerged during the rescue phase within an analytical, territorial, and participative framework.
- To activate an analytical dialogue on the study and intevention in question.
- To rescue, channel, contextualize, and encourage the ideas and proposals for regenerating the urban neighborhood.
- To integrate the results and proposals of the process in a shared document that will initiate a sociospatial transformation.

This natural disaster led us to reflect on the importance of some decisions we had taken before the crisis. In an earlier chapter we discussed our approach to various projects, such as our own offices, which makes us not simply the pilot residents of the building that we develop but also neighbors within the barrios where we work.

**The value of recognizing ourselves as neighbors and agents of transformation had never been so clear as during the aftermath of the earthquake. We become co-responsible for responding to the crisis, precisely because we were fully involved in the neighborhood.**

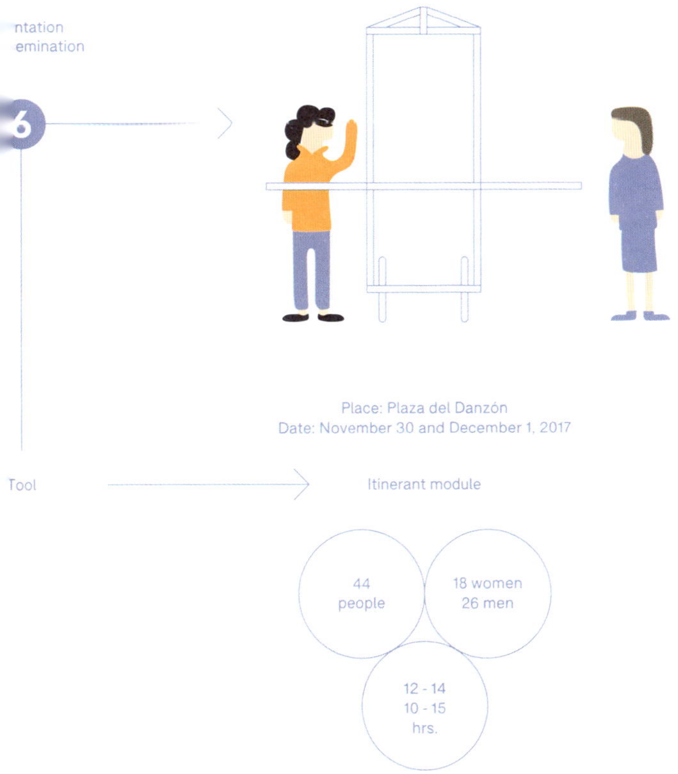

Another example we could discuss is the "Street Systems" project that started out with the intention of understanding and empathizing with informal street activities. In that case, we focused on the community living at the intersection of the Roma and Milán streets in the Juárez neighborhood. The reasons for this private use of a public space are infinitely complex, and we saw the need to raise social awareness about the various underlying systems and situations.

As a team we learned how to show tolerance and empathy toward the community, that at that time was just beside our office at Milán 44. We noticed that after we became accustomed to passing them every day, no one really looked at them. Why is it so easy to normalize precariousness and social inequalities? We put the situation on the table and began a productive dialogue about something that should not go unnoticed.

# Blurring the Boundaries: Life Outside the Projects

ReUrbano's projects do not exist solely within their interiors, they also spill out onto the streets, blurring the boundaries between public and private space. We actively seek to stimulate activities right outside buildings, constituting a clear intention and strategy behind every project.

The idea is not about putting a few tables outside but acknowledging that the street belongs to everyone and that by activating it we help increase the safety and enjoyment for citizens walking along the sidewalks. This makes a building's exterior a liminal space for its residents—an extension for the interior activities and, for those outside, a welcoming gesture.

*The Milán 44 building is porous: there are no doors or clear boundaries between interior and exterior. You are just as likely to find its residents working inside its offices as on a table on the sidewalk, while the ground-floor businesses provide a service throughout the day to inquisitive customers.*

**What type of experiences to Mexico City's buildings create? What lifestyles do they promote?**

# Confronting Regulations

# Confronting Regulations

Gabriela Etchegaray

If one principle could sum up ReUrbano, it would be its insistence on making its projects coherent with a specific model of city, one that is sustainable, rational, dynamic, fair, walkable and community-based.

A symbol of the ReUrbano model is its struggle to plan buildings without parking spaces, in a bid to help create healthier cities designed for its inhabitants, even though such developments might once have contravened regulations and therefore been unviable. ReUrbano found a solution by choosing to work on listed buildings, which were exempt from the requirement to include a minimum number of parking spaces. However, assessing these buildings' potential to transform urban environments makes investing a more complicated and drawn-out process, increasing risk and uncertainty when planning projects designed to create the desired city. This has deterred investors from becoming involved in projects that, due to regulations and the *status quo*, seem to be more focused on the common good than on the bottom line of the investor's portfolio.

> **Citizens, private investors, and government authorities must collaborate to build up a consensus about the type of city that is desirable and worthwhile over the long term.**

For ReUrbano, accompaniment means guaranteeing the interaction of various groups, by considering local versus floating populations, mixed-use housing and rent stabilization programs, the importance of preserving traditions, and support for local businesses.

The only way to achieve this commitment to accompaniment is by not viewing building developments solely as business opportunities, an approach that can have a detrimental effect on neighborhoods. David Harvey's remark that cities cannot be a place for investment, but a place in which to live gives meaning to this vision. Therefore, it would seem logical to avoid repeating past mistakes and instead support small-scale real-estate developers more willing to innovate and take risks with a view to improving the city. Therefore urban and fiscal policies and regulations must be responsible in order to provide greater benefits to compensate the risks and difficulties incurred by those working for society's benefit.

However, current administrative processes are not conducive for small investor groups. Although it is true that until the 1990s the state played the role of investor and regulator, the relentless drive of neoliberalism has turned the city's real-estate development sector into a predominantly private enterprise since the state lost its power as urban regulator. Contrary to appearances, it would have no reason to avoid becoming more involved in a better model of city; it could implement regulatory and fiscal incentives to reward urban initiatives favoring higher-risk strategies that go against the *status quo* in order

**ReUrbano has worked with a self-imposed (urban) model that has been taking shape over the past ten years, gradually consolidating a better city for everyone in the near future.**

to benefit the community, unlike the current situation. Such initiatives could include rent stabilization, sustainable social amenities, support for local businesses, and the integral preservation of heritage properties.

To achieve this, ReUrbano applies sustainability criteria, fosters social cohesion between programs and users, and ensures that projects are feasible and have solid financial foundations. But states also must also play an instrumental role to help create a better city. The lack of an urban model implies the absence of urban strategies. This gives rise to an alarming, widespread feeling that complying with regulations does not always mean meeting these objectives, and also fails to create a better, greener, friendlier, or fairer city. A city—formed by institutions and citizens—must know and agree to be co-responsible for what it wants and needs to be. This will reduce uncertainty when opting for a given project, on the basis of whether or not it will contribute to a jointly desired city model. These ideas form the basis of the urgent need for joining up public policies with investors who provide the financing.

**For ReUrbano, "to develop" is a verb that means intervening on a property over the long term. It starts with identifying the place, performing a diagnosis, drawing up an architectural design, and planning uses and activities in an uninterrupted accompaniment over the project's lifespan.**

Should this support the existence of local, small, and medium-sized real-estate developers? This would be a legitimate means of balancing the scales for the investor—a balance required to offer returns while minimizing risks as far as possible, at the same time as offering incentives designed to create a city more like the one we want, even if it is not the most profitable in the short term.

The government needs to set up a system of regulatory, legal, and fiscal incentives to create rental premises for local businesses; it should preserve heritage properties discretionally. This would sustain activities that private investors would otherwise shun, create a greener city, and share open spaces more safely and generously. ReUrbano has already carried out similar initiatives on a small scale, but a collaboration with local authorities would create a more balanced urban environment. Making these management models scalable requires evidence that working on pre-existing structures with the support of local citizens private property can be compatible with public projects in the city of the future.

# Translating the Regulations: The DNA of a Built Environment

**CoRe provides a space where various key players in urban development can meet, exchange ideas, and reach agreements.**

Developers usually approach urban regulations solely with a view to maximizing profit and these same regulations are inaccessible for those affected by them. How can regular citizens question and have an impact on regulations without fully understanding them?

At their most basic level, we understand regulations as a series of variables and restrictions applicable to real-estate projects ideally inserted within a neighborhood. We also believe that they should be entirely logical and provide a blueprint for the best city possible. Unfortunately, they almost invariably fall short of such expectations.

For example, why do regulations not provide a stimulus for building more homes provided that they are affordable? Where are the incentives to contribute to public space to make them more energy efficient? And to create dignified jobs and to consider not only the future inhabitants of a building but also the rest of the community. For those who believe this is too much to ask, let us reiterate: we need to ask for much more, and that will only be possible by empowering the population by giving them access to greater knowledge.

To this end, in 2016 we founded CoRe, an association that seeks to democratize the existing information on the city's urban laws and regulations by translating concepts that are usually impenetrable.

CoRe

UNA
CIUDAD
DE
DISTANCIAS
CORTAS
CoRe
AÑO 3

# Extreme Regulations: Protesting with Proposals

We realize that proposing alternatives t urban realities without understanding th regulations in force is impossible. Howeve we also recognize that many regulations ar obsolete and no longer relevant to the city' current needs.

Therefore, stakeholders need to collab rate to make an impact and they must que tion the regulations in order to bring them u to date. Looking to the future, we need to as ourselves:

---

**The state's role is to create regulations and incentives to encourage the type of city we want, rather than simply prohibiting the one we do not want.**

---

It is impossible to propose alternatives to the current situation without having a grasp of the underlying regulations.

What do the city's public spaces require to become more accessible and safer?

How can we ensure that new developments have a sustainable ecological footprint?

Which responsibilities should be established around renewable energy?

Mexico City's regulatory framework is clearly out of step with the 21st century. Looking to the future, we must ask ourselves:

How can we deal with floods in a city that also suffers water shortages?

What measures can we take to reduce traffic and long car journeys?

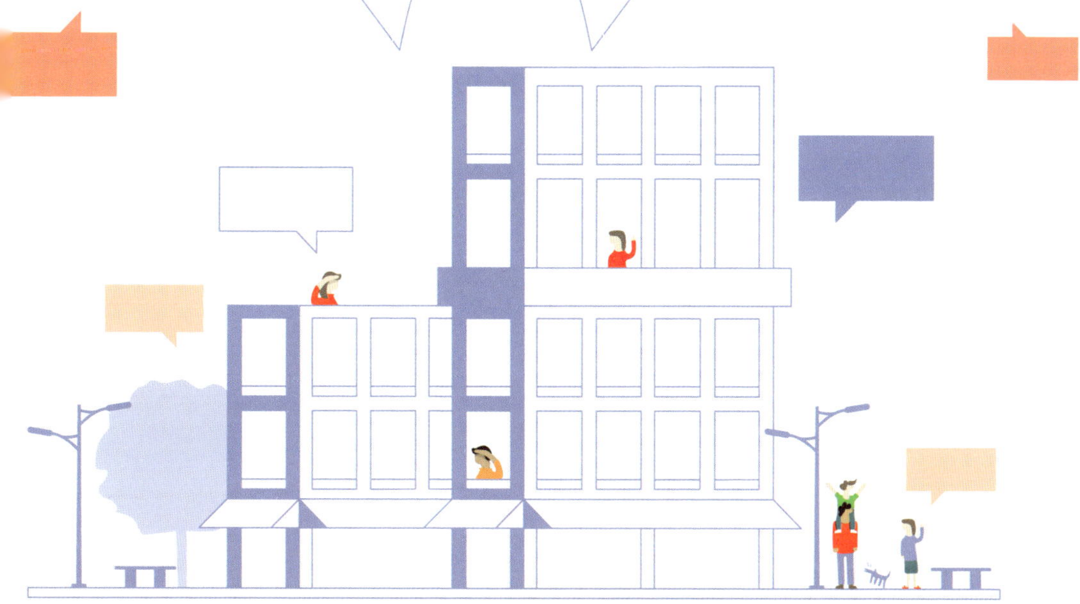

# Other Regulations: Alternatives to Certain Gaps in Regulations

A proposal of some alterations or additions to the regulations in order to establish the right legal conditions for the ideal 21st-century city. Government authorities and regulatory bodies should:

1. Establish suitable rents for all kinds of income in the same sector, whether a property, a specific area or a neighborhood in order to ensure a diverse society and cultural wealth, and to strike an economic balance. This would require a proportioal distribution by income bands, ensuring that each sector or area includes homes for different social classes.

2. Commit to incentivize urban policies, targeted at stakeholder and developer groups who invest in urban transformation, in order to encourage investors to commit to developing the city in a positive way.

3 Promote tax incentives to help mitigate the risks borne by promoters of projects that are beneficial for the urban environment. These projects must be justified socially and economically, either by forming an integral part of the community and having a positive impact because their spaces are shared or by preventing the creation of ghettos.

4 Ensure discretionality in regulating urban developments. The possibility of adjusting and applying flexible conditions in regulations, meeting the needs of each area of the city and each property. The adjustments of the regulation should be based on a prior assessment of the urban impact, of the arguments in favor of specific treatment or analysis by the local authorities of the area in question, considering its historic, social, economic and heritage value.

5 Include a requirement of an impact assessment for all urban development projects. This evaluation must justify and foresee the consequences of the project within its context. An urban impact assessment includes the prior collection and mapping out of urban data and uses, as well as the study of the acceptance and integration of the project within its surroundings.

6 Regulate the percentage of the free area ceded for public use according to the criteria officially considered as public space. This regulation promotes the ceding of open spaces and generous inclusions within public space, reducing the promoter's responsibility in terms of actions beyond its control within the ceded free space.

7 Establish a system of fiscal incentives before promoting and protecting rental premises for local businesses. Select, follow up, and monitor small businesses that can access these rent-controlled premises. This measure will benefit local businesses, strengthen small enterprises, and promote entrepreneurship among local residents.

# Community Inclusion: Active Listening

For ReUrbano, generating models of community inclusion during the various phases of our projects is necessary both to gain an understanding of the neighborhood and its residents and to increase internal and external accountability on a continual basis.

Creating these models of participation does not simply mean opening up a space to canvass views from locals. We have had to learn to document, present, receive, listen, interview and design genuine encounters. These exchanges inform and improve our work, but it is important to highlight the need for local authorities also to play an active role in the processes of citizen participation; social dynamics should not be the sole responsibility of private developers. Everyone is responsible for requiring the authorities' involvement.

**Citizen participation is essential for the development of any city, neighborhood, or project that fulfils the needs and wishes of the community in question.**

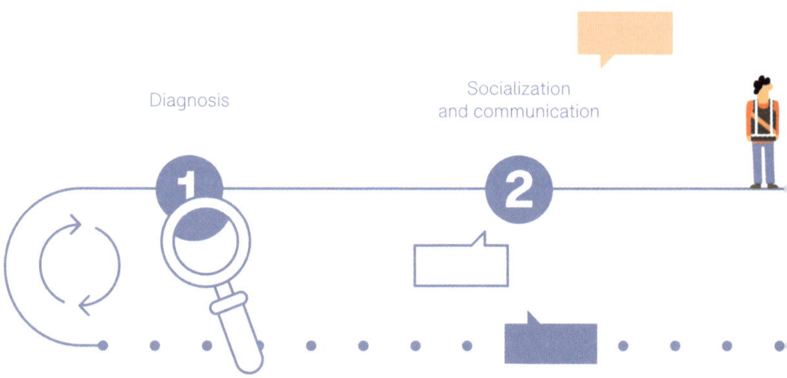

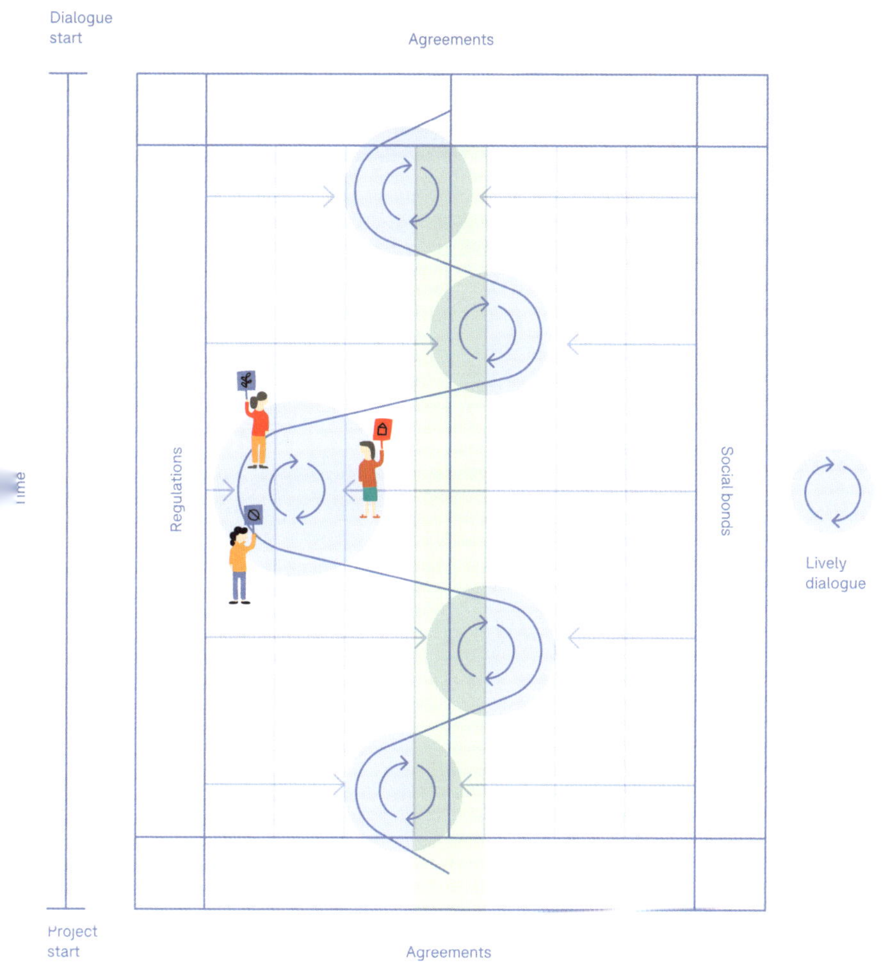
Dialogue
start
Agreements
Time
Regulations
Social bonds
Lively
dialogue
Project
start
Agreements

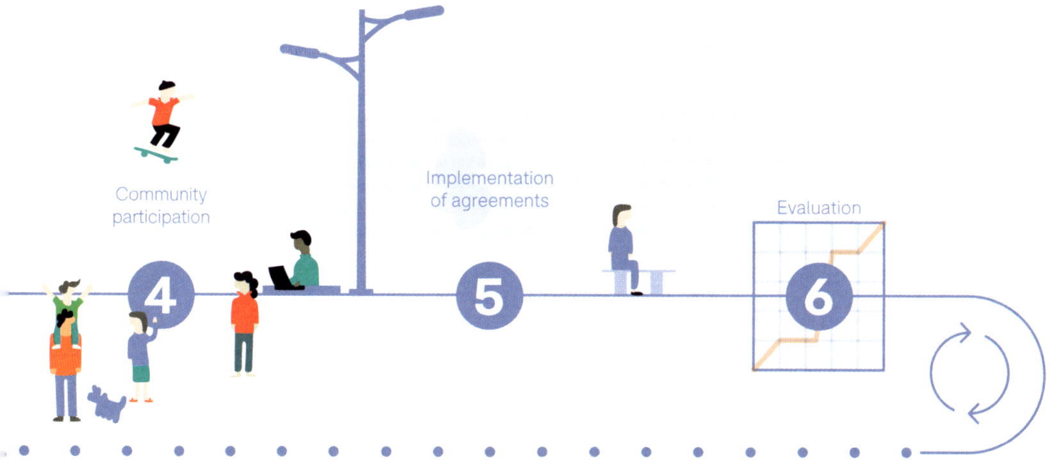
Community
participation
4
Implementation
of agreements
5
Evaluation
6

# Experimenting and Interlinking: Maps and Proposals

We are a real-estate developer. We are not a real-estate developer.

Our methodology is not simply about a building's profitability, aesthetics, or use. It measures its impact on the surrounding context: the sidewalk, the street, the activity on both; whether its occupants will increase or decrease traffic or whether our businesses create and contribute or extract and transfer wealth.

In order to determine how we can make an impact on generating positive neighborhood dynamics, we set up an internal database that seeks to identify areas of potential improvement and urban growth in the public space. Our team constantly adds to this database. Internally we refer to it the "project calculator," as a resource that keeps us focused on priorities, mapping key stakeholders and potential proposals.

That is our philosophy and our roadmap. The result is visible and we can discuss it as something tangible—it is created and delivered to the city to trigger a wide-ranging conversation about the urban life to which everyone aspires, not only in ReUrbano or among our clients, partners, and collaborators

**Ɔur work constantly fluctuates between these ɔontradictory ideas. We see our work going ɔeyond the limits of development and we avoid ɔlassifications. We are a multidisciplinary real-ɘstate platform, an urban laboratory experimenting vith ideas that reflect our vision for the city.**

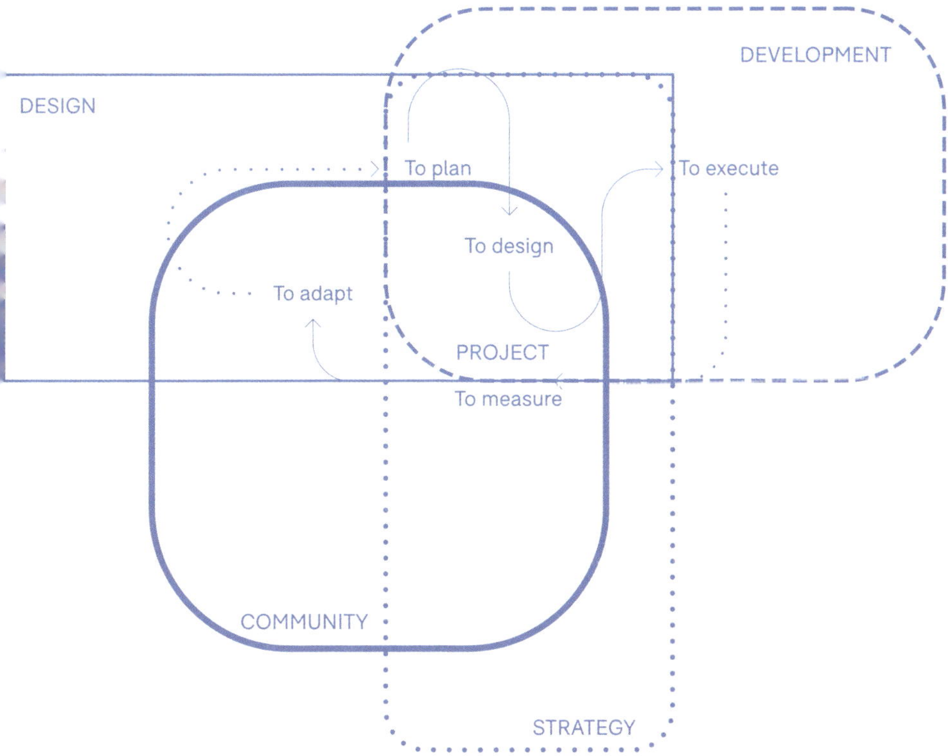

# Affordable Housing: One of Many Routes Toward Inclusion

*Less waste, greater affordability.*

This means that we should reduce urban waste—empty lots, abandoned buildings, unused public spaces—in order to develop affordable housing and socially diverse neighborhoods.

We have realized that "legal" and "legitimate" are not necessarily synonymous. The urban improvements implemented in Mexico City's central neighborhoods have not benefitted every socioeconomic sector and the city continues to suffer from a housing shortage. ReUrbano is committed to the challenge of integrating affordable housing into our developments.

We have explored ways of creating developments for mixed socioeconomic levels. In this way, members of a community who face the risk of displacement can still have access to high-quality, affordable housing.

However, developers' good intentions will only go so far for this to cause a genuine impact and for this working model not only to be viable but also scalable. This objective requires a genuine commitment from the relevant local authorities as they can adjust regulations to create the right conditions to activate other forms of inclusion.

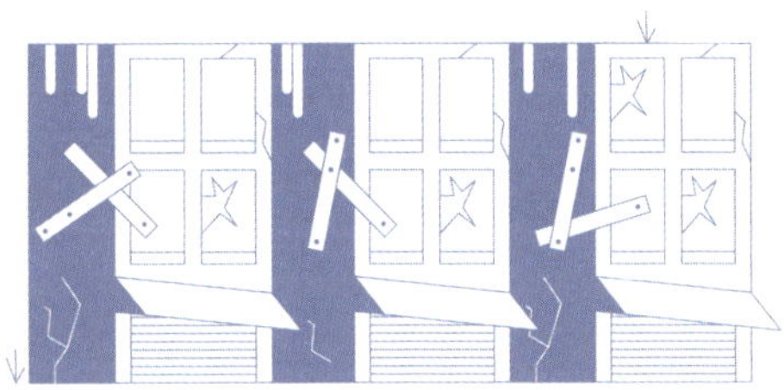

In 2010, there were 5 million abandoned dwellings

1. To recover the property

2. To implement affordable housing rent ≤ 30% of the incomes

3. To include commercial premises in the ground floor

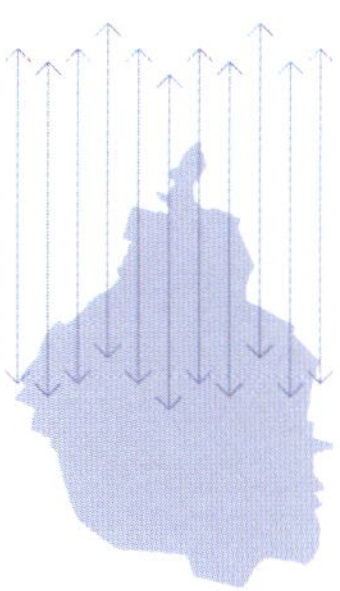

5 million people cross the border between the State of Mexico and Mexico City every day

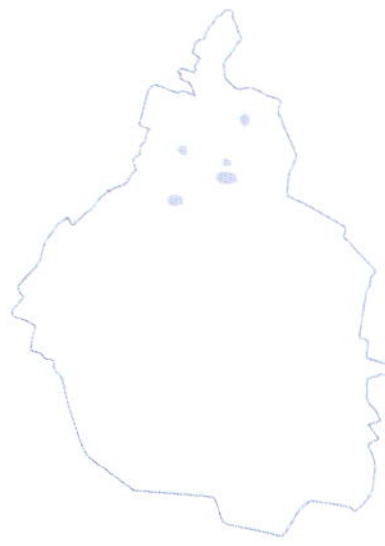

1467

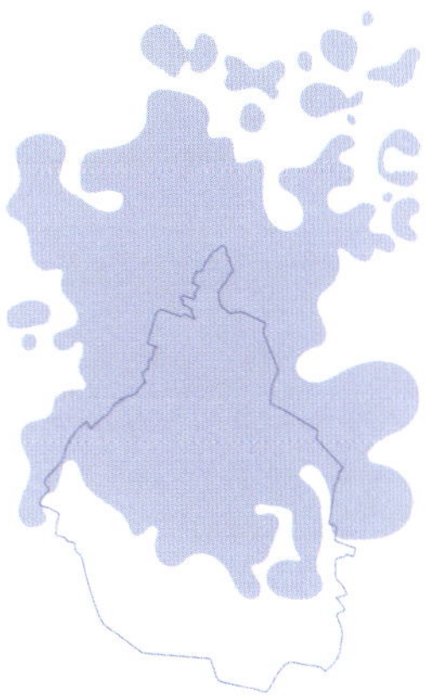

2000

# The Value of Design

# The Value of Design

Gabriela Etchegaray

Design is present in all that we perceive, and its reach is even as broad as humanity itself. And although we could see design as a service for human beings, it often *redesigns* humans by modifying our way of living and our customs. The reason for this could be that it does the opposite of other professional disciplines that look for causes in the past.

Nevertheless, the action of designing does not foresee the future. Instead it presupposes the responsibility of the use of a product over time: What will be the effects of its use and the consequences of its implementation in the market, the city, the neighborhood, the user. And, if it is true that design is a tool that creates a future—a desirable future—then how can we evaluate its results? How can we be sure that design will create a better future? Evaluating results cannot and must not only depend on objective parameters such as financial considerations. On this premise, ReUrbano also bases its work on subjective values that are hard to quantify yet equally universal, and are shared by a broad majority, and these can acquire a greater weight than the objective values of the common good.

**Design tries to previsualize something that does not yet exist but that should be carefully considered before bringing it into existence.**

**ReUrbano understands that the design process requires time, to rethink present and future consequences, to untangle processes that control decision-making, and to mark the boundaries of design, conscious of the involvement of users and the community.**

When considering the scale of values for a "good" design, we need to establish an axiological code—a series of self-imposed assessment criteria that could also be shared by anyone creating a design that seeks to achieve a more responsible practice. Emiliano Godoy encourages us to use straightforward criteria to assess our projects by setting parameters; a good design needs to be environmentally regenerative, socially fair, functionally innovative, politically active, economically distributive, symbolically progressive, technologically evolutionary, culturally relevant, and ultimately create desirable futures.

**Simply by understanding the role of design *in the future*—with the contribution of processes rather than closed responses—design can determine actions as conscious tools for positive transformations.**

This code combines subjective and quantitative parameters in order to point to a desirable future, assuming that design has an effect that goes beyond the finished object. ReUrbano proposes that 21st-century design should no longer place so much weight on the ends and focus instead on the *means*. Although the end product has an intrinsic value, that value is connected to the means with which that end was reached.

For ReUrbano this interpretation defines citizenship. By adopting this attitude, we prioritize the process above the object, turning on its head the classic approach to design as a means to resolve a problem. Design in the 21st century is dynamic and therefore cannot provide fixed, static, and lasting solutions. Instead these solutions are shifting and depend on the temporal context in which they have been established. The problem-solution dichotomy lacks all of the subtleties inherent in the design of today's world; it is insufficient to explain it. The moment may have come to assume that a "good" design does not respond to a brief but to another question that triggers processes that change the way of thinking and secure a better outcome for everyone.

No longer is it enough to expect professionalism and concise answers from designers, architects, promoters of the contemporary city, or even from citizens. We now need to add a critical sense of responsibility and awareness where the materialization of works has an impact as an integral part of a much broader network. Therefore, the question is not merely about *what* is being designed, but *how*: What are the processes, what working structure is used for the study, and what will be the role of citizen participation? Simply by understanding the role of design *in the future*—with the contribution of processes rather than closed responses—design can determine actions as conscious tools for positive transformations.

# Weaving the City: Block by Block

For ReUrbano, “design” is not a concept only applied to something formal and tangible, but instead a mentality that exists on the many different scales of our business model, ranging from the building, the sidewalk, the block, the neighborhood and ultimately the city.

Each scale, in its own way, focuses its efforts on users, which is both the individual and society, in order to design a city that makes an impact on the human and the environment

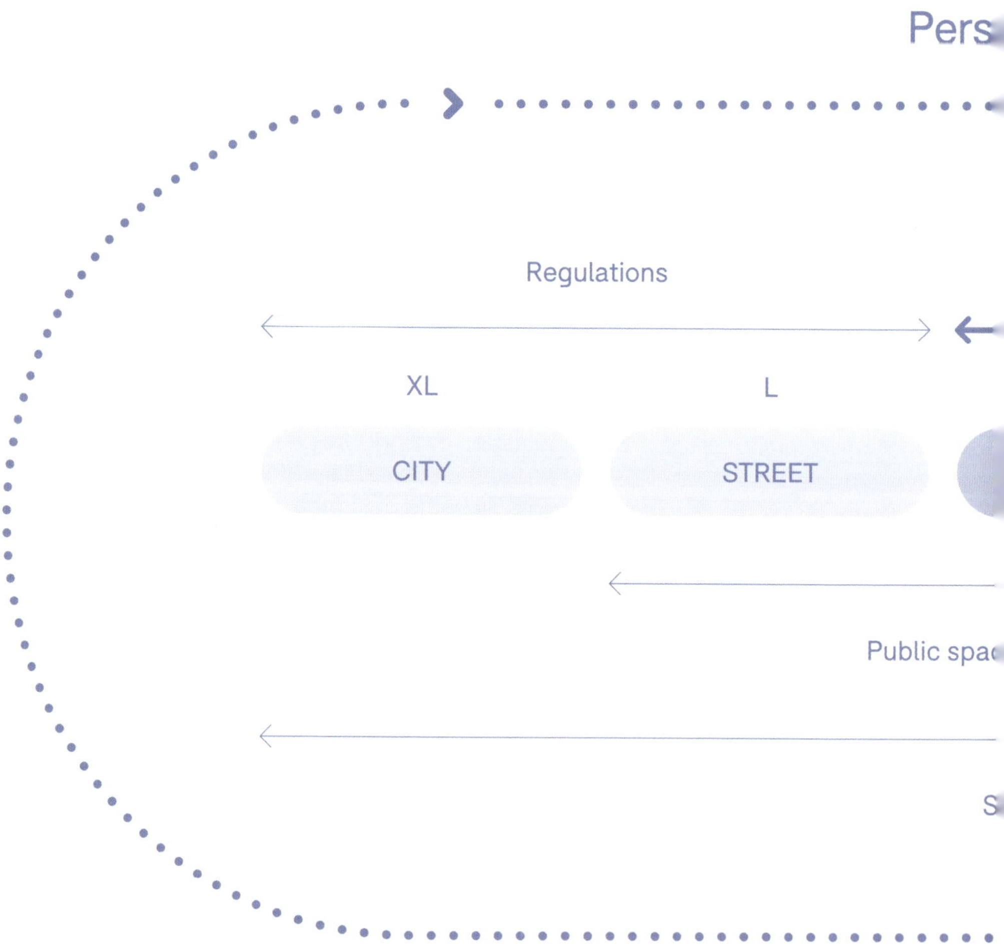

# lation

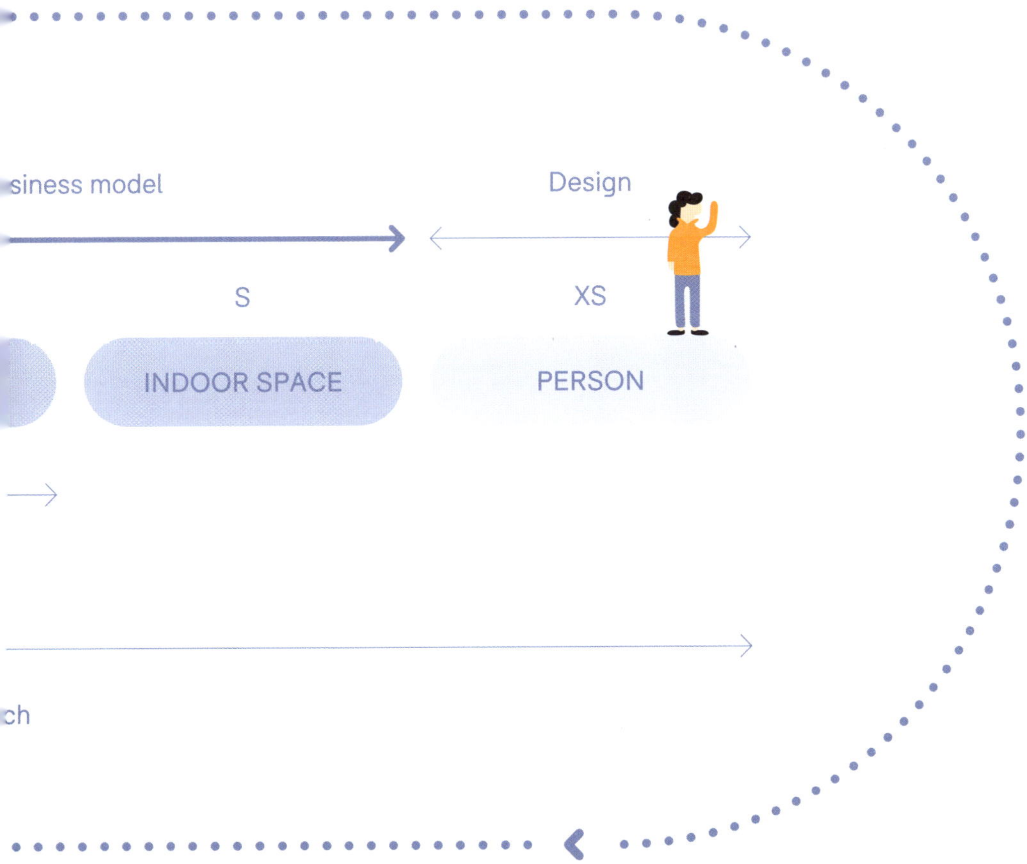

# What, How, and Why: Different Approaches and Perspectives

How do we do it?

We start out with the idea of putting ourselves "in the other person's shoes." In order to understand the world from someone else's perspective, you need to involve that "other" person. The biologist, the sociologist, the educator, the businessperson, the urban designer, the economist, the engineer—they all see the city through a different prism, and these approaches make it possible for us to create a more complete vision of the city that exists for everyone's benefit.

In particular, ReUrbano's working model involves systematic collaborations with various architecture and design studios, as well as people working in the arts, academia, institutions, business, as well as the residents and neighbors of our developments.

These processes do not simply produce another building; each one gives lessons and experiences. In the case of the city, criticism and research must become actions. We know that no course of action is infallible. We have a strong belief in the power of ideas, both our own and those of others.

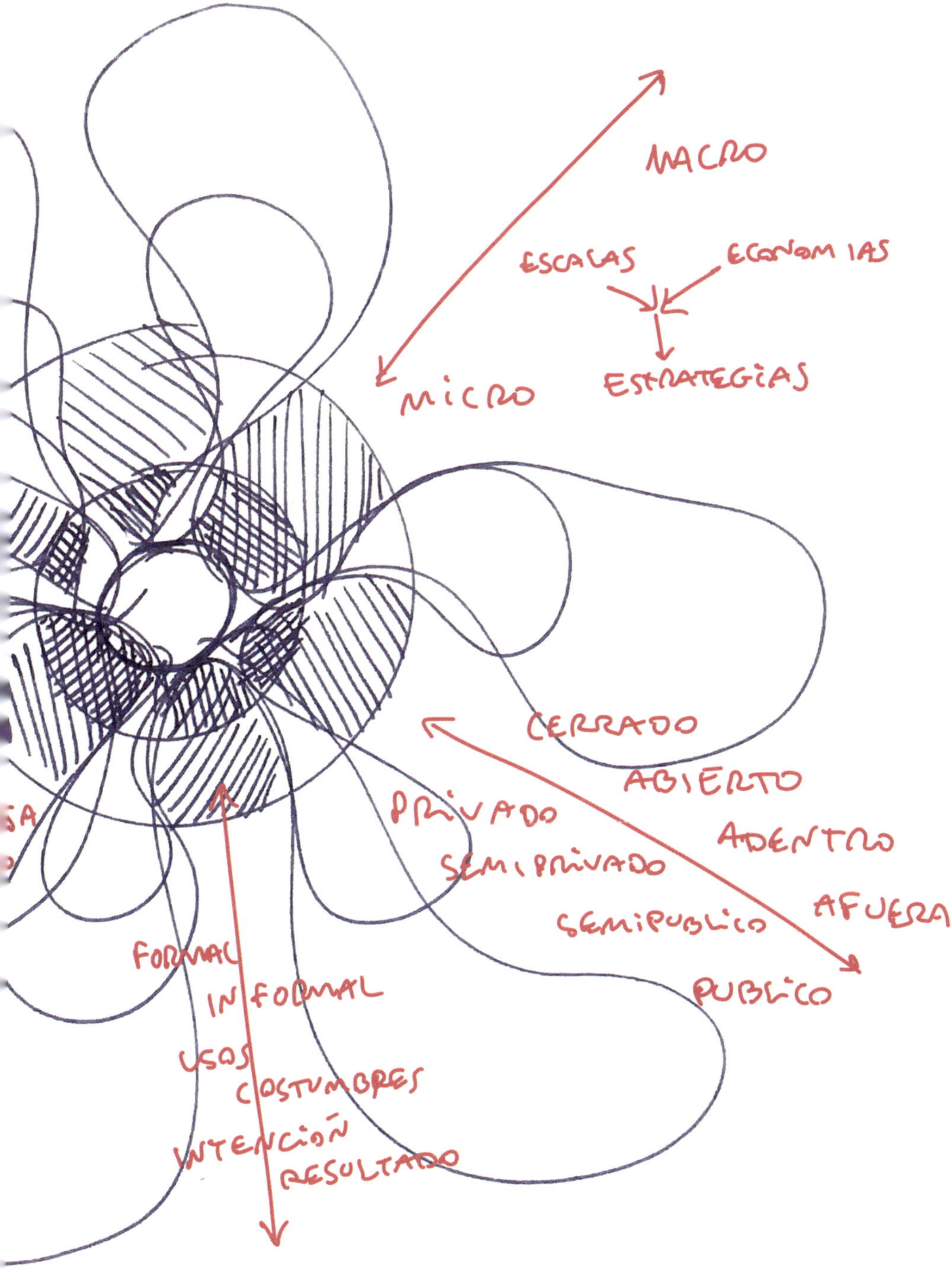
MACRO
ESCALAS
ECONOMIAS
ESTRATEGIAS
MICRO
CERRADO
ABIERTO
ADENTRO
AFUERA
PRIVADO
SEMIPRIVADO
SEMIPUBLICO
PUBLICO
FORMAL
INFORMAL
USOS
COSTUMBRES
INTENCIÓN
RESULTADO

# Integrating Every Element: Present, Past, Future

When we talk about integrated design, we are not only thinking about restoring or reviving buildings or areas, but taking into account their future uses and how these connect to the history of their neighborhoods.

*La Laguna was built as a large textile factory. With some modifications to adapt it to the current market, we managed to preserve the character of the building that now houses several smaller production workshops.*

*The structure of Milán 44 changed from being a auto parts warehouse to a vibrant building, with ground-floor stores that activated the street and workspaces on the upper floors.*

*Havre 77 was formerly a perfumery and then a veterinary clinic before eventually being turned into a building of offices and restaurants that is now a hub of local neighborhood activity.*

*The neighboring building, Havre 69, was initially the site of four mansions that we adapted to make 14 apartments, a bakery and a café.*

Each ReUrbano project has both a formal and practical design. The city is gradually adapting to its citizens' new lifestyles. Part of our mission is to understand previous uses in order to plan for present and future ones.

BUNA

# Multiscale Model: When Everything Makes an Impact

**We activate a particular point that triggers change from a micro to a macro level.**

Our intention to create a community with shared values within building developments is scalable: in other words, it can spread beyond the confines of a building to link together various similar projects close to one another. The corridors mentioned throughout this book seek to bond communities that underlie urban infrastructure networks and support certain ways of living in the 21st century.

The model—which works block by block—can be applied subsequently neighborhood by neighborhood, and finally city by city. Though not a new idea, it is something that can be readapted on a case-by-case basis. We are not the first and we hope not to be the last.

Ten years ago we began with one building. We followed up with another one. Eventually we developed a couple of city blocks through specific, interconnected interventions. We are now planning on a more ambitious scale through urban corridors, seeking to bring together more stakeholders, more buildings with more public space, in order to make a greater positive impact.

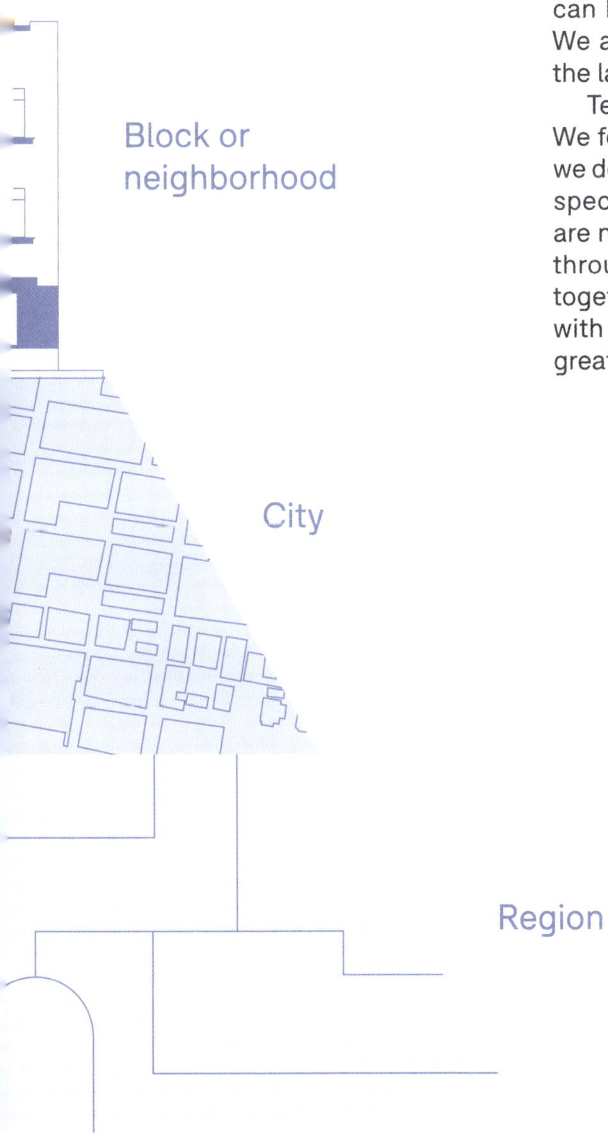

# Introspection: Rethinking Interior Boundaries

We think that the best boundary is one that is not easily noticeable, one built out of respect, negotiations, and agreements. The interior space is private, intimate, a place for shelter and reflection, and also where we welcome others to get to know us. Each limit or opening, each open or closed space, each transition, is impregnated with meaning when we inhabit a space.

When designing a project, we ask ourselves: Once you're outside, what will be the impact of having entered? Who are you on the inside, and who are you on the outside?

The user's experience inside a building depends on both physical and social factors. Who feels welcome in a space, and who does not? How can you design the interior of a building to make it flexible and inclusive?

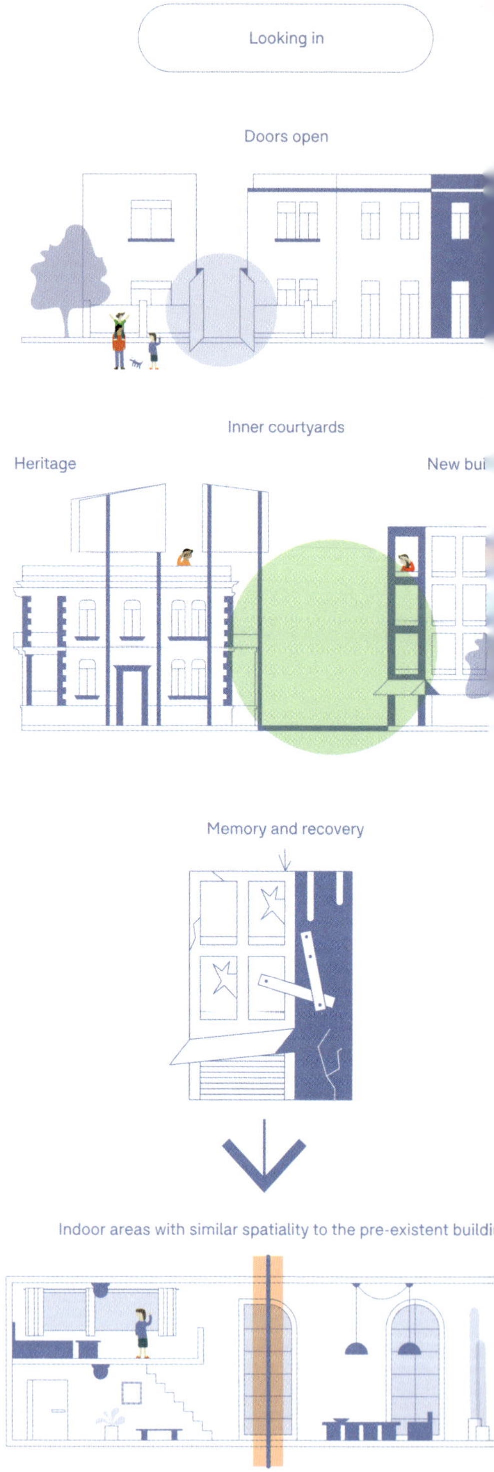

# Extrospection: Joining the Outdoors

“Inside” and “outside” are mental constructs that are projected in a building. A building’s boundaries and the ways of living represent its creator’s way of thinking and unveil his or her ideology and values.

Including or excluding, welcoming or expelling, embracing or rejecting. Each building does this to the urban public space and therefore to neighbors and other citizens. We ask again: What kind of city do we want?

How can we design spaces that blur the boundaries between the interior and exterior?

What tangible and intangible elements create inclusive ambiences from out on the street?

Looking out

BALCONIES

COMMUNICATION

Open façade

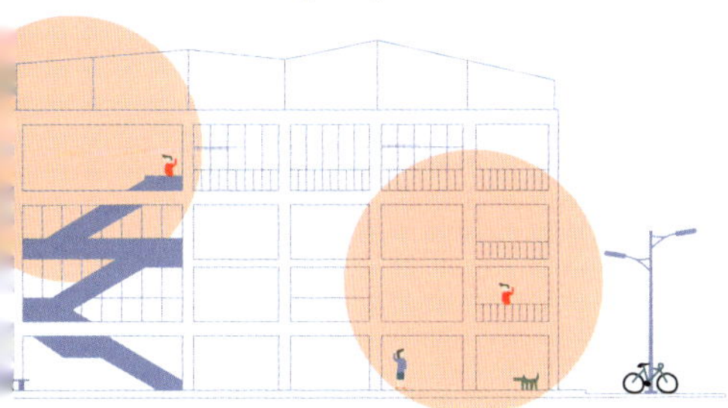

VEGETATION OUTSIDE THE BUILDING

# Building Common Spaces on the Foundations of Working Groups, Dialogue, and Social Interactions

This book is ultimately a process of self-analysis, of looking within and outside Reurbano; it is about identifying, analyzing, and understanding our impact on Mexico City over the past decade, and our potential impact in the next ten years. And, like every other one, this process was possible thanks to a series of dialogues with our collaborators, specialists, consultants, partners, critics, communities and neighbors who have enriched our work up to now, and with whom we hope to continue to collaborate on designing a more sustainable city in the future.

continuidad

PENSAMIENTO OBJETO PERSONA
AQUÍ ESTUVE YO COSA
MEMORIA NEGOCIADO PREEXISTENCIA
HERENCIA CONTEXTO LA MEMORIA NO ES ESTABLE PARTICIPACIÓN
TIEMPO
COLECTIVO CAMBIO INTANGIBLE
PRESERVACIÓN OBJETO HUELLA
CAMBIO
AGUA HISTORIA. bicicleta o aprendizaje de andar en ella. USO ECOSISTEMA
APRENDIZAJE
URBANO PAISAJE LIBERTAD CARACTERÍSTICAS
CIUDAD REGLAS REVERSIBLE ¿PERMANENTE? ACUPUNTURA
sociedad. DINAMICAS ARCHIPIELAGO

LREU
15. Ago. 2019
AK.

MÁS O MENOS ARQUITECTURA?

¿QUÉ PASARÍA SI LO QUE PROTEGEMOS ES EL ESPACIO?
¿CÓMO LOGRAS PONER EL EJEMPLO? (ROMPIENDO LAS REGLAS)
¿Y CON EL EJEMPLO, CAMBIAR LAS REGLAS?

..Y SI ES TERRENO VALDÍO?

"SIEMPRE HAY UNA PRE-EXISTENCIA"

→ Koolhaas "Fuck the context"
EL contexto incendió su edificio en CHINA (juegos pirotécnicos)

ESQUELETO
ES ATEMPORAL
Y LA PIEL?
PIELES EXÓTICAS
piel = apariencia
maquillaje
cosmética.

VENECIA: cual de los pasados debería rescatar? preservar? (...fosilizar?).

# Projects

Bucareli 80

Chihuahua 139

Córdoba 125

Emilio Castelar 22

Emilio Dondé 7

Emilio Dondé 68

Havre 69

Havre 77

Havre 83

Iztaccíhuatl 54

La Laguna

Liverpool 9

Milán 44

Manuel Dublán 46

Sindicalismo 76

Versalles 84

Zamora 15

# Bucareli 80

Location
Bucareli 80
Colonia Centro

Distance to public space
230 meters,
Plaza del Danzón

Distance to public transport station
650 meters,
M Balderas

Parking spaces
0

Year
2015 - Under construction

Heritage list
INBAL, INAH

Record of previous uses
Magic supplies store
Auto repair
Bicycle store

Current use
Commercial + residential

Percentage / $m^2$ recovered
97% / 13,750 $m^2$

Partner architect
MMX

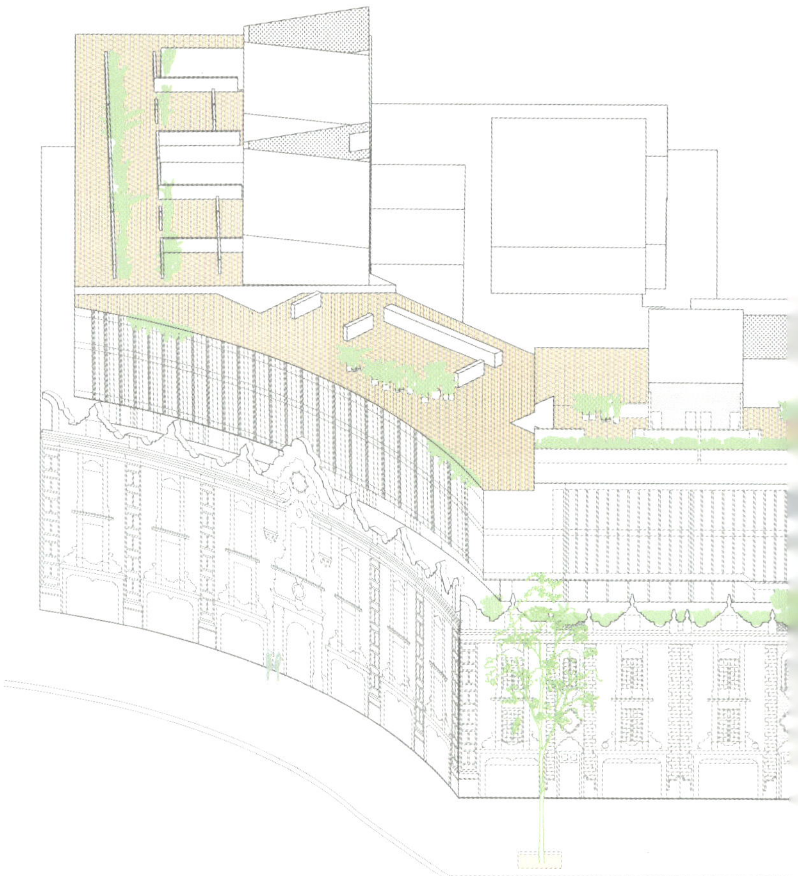

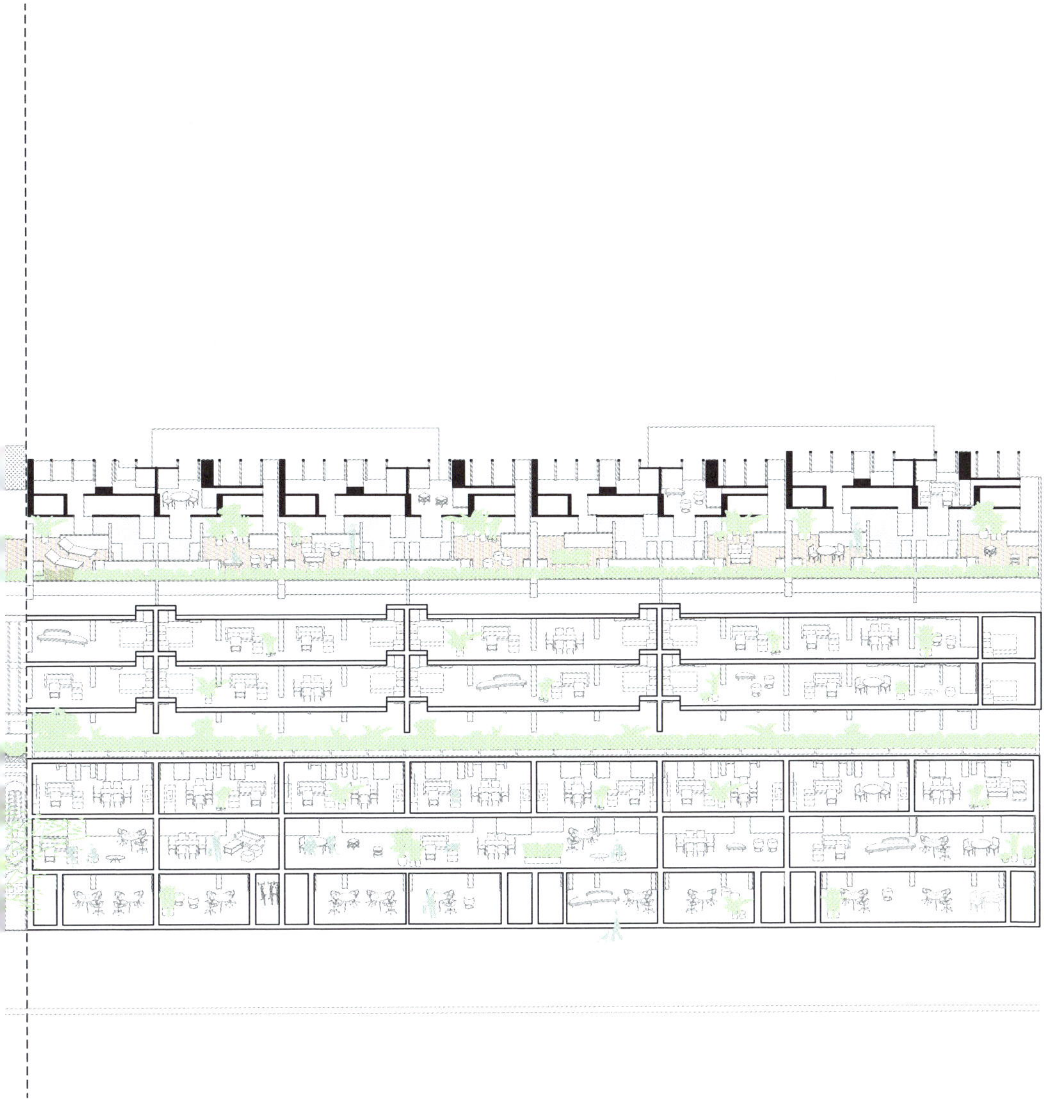

The bullfighter Rodolfo Gaona commissioned the architect Ángel Torres Torrija to design and build the Gaona building in the early 20th century.

This is one of the earliest examples of the few mixed, multi-family developments built for the middle classes. One of the building's characteristic features are the clearly distinguishable stages in the various construction materials and systems, allowing us to clearly identify and differentiate them.

The oldest section corresponds to the part of the building on Calle Emilio Dondé. The second stage of construction stretches roughly 35 meters from the cantered wall down Avenida Bucareli.

The third stage corresponds to a volume measuring approximately 60 meters long on the same avenue. Although this emulates the same style as the previous stage, we can appreciate concrete elements on the windows with polylobate arches, and on the jambs dividing each groove. Instead of the stone construction elements, we used prepoured concrete elements that imitate the finished quality, textures, and colors of the stone.

The fourth and final stage corresponds to the interior body, the construction systems based on pre-assembled reinforced concrete slabs, beams and upright supports with buttresses that reveal an interval of several decades after the previous stage.

---

## LEARNINGS

This kind of remodeling project presents complex challenges, requiring a larger effort than when starting from zero. Apart from the architectural design itself, other factors came into play. We learned how to establish links to government institutions such as INBAL, INAH and SEDUVI, and how to promote the rescue of listed buildings. It is important to respect what already exists and also create new dynamics before embarking on a project in the areas both inside and outside the building.

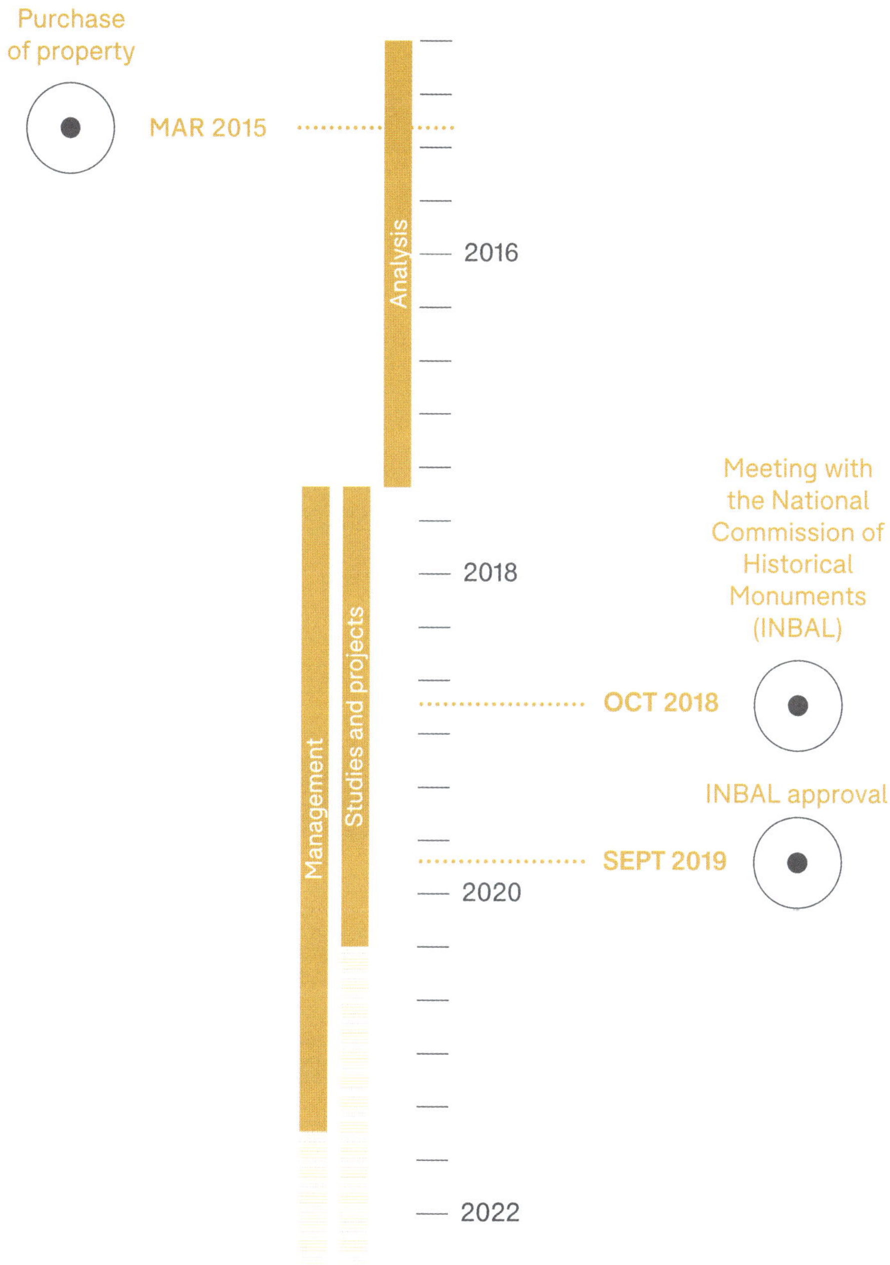
Purchase
of property
MAR 2015
Analysis
2016
Management
Studies and projects
2018
Meeting with
the National
Commission of
Historical
Monuments
(INBAL)
OCT 2018
INBAL approval
SEPT 2019
2020
2022

MAGO CHAMS
MAGO
CHAMS

# Chihuahua 139

Location
Chihuahua 139
Colonia Roma

Distance to public space
240 meters,
Plaza Luis Cabrera

Distance to public transport station
500 meters,
MB Álvaro Obregón

Parking spaces
0

Year
2013 - 2015

Heritage list
INBAL

Record of previous uses
Grocery store

Current use
Commercial + residential

Percentage / m² recovered
85% / 1,650 m²

Partner architect
Cadaval & Solà-Morales

This building exemplifies our ambitions for 21st-century cities by integrating a blend of different uses and services.

Chihuahua 139 included services ranging from a (pre-existing) fruiterer to an Enrique Olvera restaurant, making it a single building with three different uses: a ground-floor store, first-floor offices, and residential units on the other levels. In order to keep the fruiterer in place, the building's owner agreed to a fixed monthly rent at the going market rate for all the premises, averaging the lease paid by the other residents to meet the expectations of the investors. ReUrbano also took on the job of designing the fruiterer's store, ensuring that he could continue working with the same inventory, although the new space was smaller.

---

**RESULT AND IMPACT**
Chihuahua 139 provided us an important case study, building our knowledge of what to do with complex projects and in locations undergoing change. Promoting businesses already in place is not only a positive way of giving local people and long-standing businesses a chance to remain but it also taught us that this approach also has a (replicable) risk-mitigation aspect.

**LEARNINGS**
This is the only project in which we have only worked as service providers; in other words, coordinating the design, architecture, program, and construction without being involved in the investment funds.

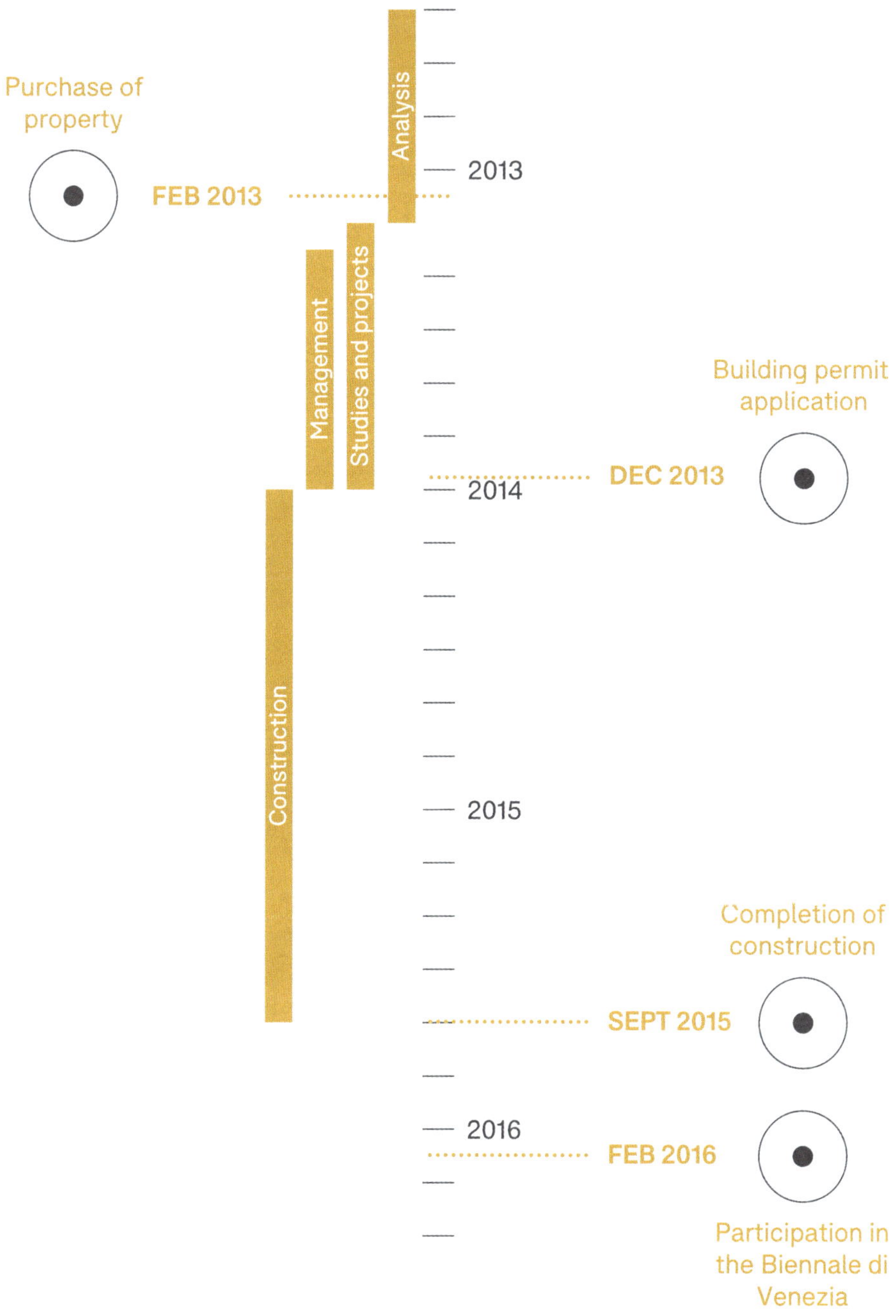
Purchase of property
FEB 2013
Analysis
2013
Management
Studies and projects
Building permit application
DEC 2013
2014
Construction
2015
Completion of construction
SEPT 2015
2016
FEB 2016
Participation in the Biennale di Venezia

Reparadora de Calzado "El Camioncito"

ABARROTES
CREMERIA

39

hel
ve
tica
hel
ve
tica
R
382

# Córdoba 125

Location
Córdoba 125
Colonia Roma

Distance to public space
240 meters,
Plaza Luis Cabrera

Distance to public transport station
260 meters, Ecobici

Parking spaces
0

Year
2011 - 2014

Heritage list
INBAL

Record of previous uses
Furniture store

Current use
Commercial + residential

Percentage / $m^2$ recovered
100% / 450 $m^2$

Partner architect
Cadaval & Solà-Morales

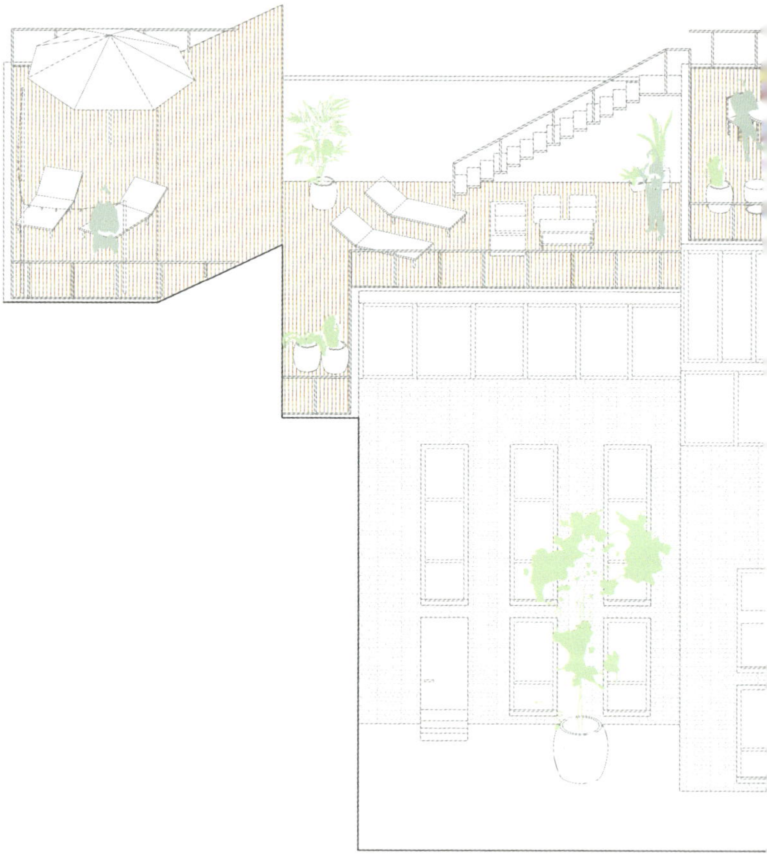

A long side passage gives Córdoba 125 its structure: the existing entrance courtyard in the original house is replicated to the rear, providing two entrance routes to the building. Emphasizing the development's horizontality, the first floor built over the pre-existing building is entirely glazed, making the extension as lightweight as possible and clearly differentiating the original structure and the intervention. The top floor is built with air and architecture: a series of terraces and built volumes alter the perception of the building's total height, and to stylize the project as a series of small volumes rather than a single solid mass.

The materials are also important. The original house is built of brick, the same material also used in the extension to the rear. The original material is rough, vibrant, laden with identity and history; the new structure distinguishes itself from the pre-existing structure in the details, from the industrial structures right down to the perforations in the walls. These subtle details make it possible to identify the differences and similarities that create a single entity. The upper-story volumes have their own personality, both due to the material itself and their color palette.

## RESULT AND IMPACT

The project's design (and high profile thanks to awards, magazine features, etc.) has a potentially positive impact on the project, which was selected for the Venice Architecture Biennial in 2016.

## LEARNINGS

We did not receive survey responses from end users to identify if the spaces encourage long-term use.

In these cases we formed a part of the influx of investment in the Roma neighborhood already taking place, and the lesson we learned was that it is good to be alert to seize opportunities to add to the portfolio. High-performing investments with greater levels of certainty are necessary for averaging and reinvesting.

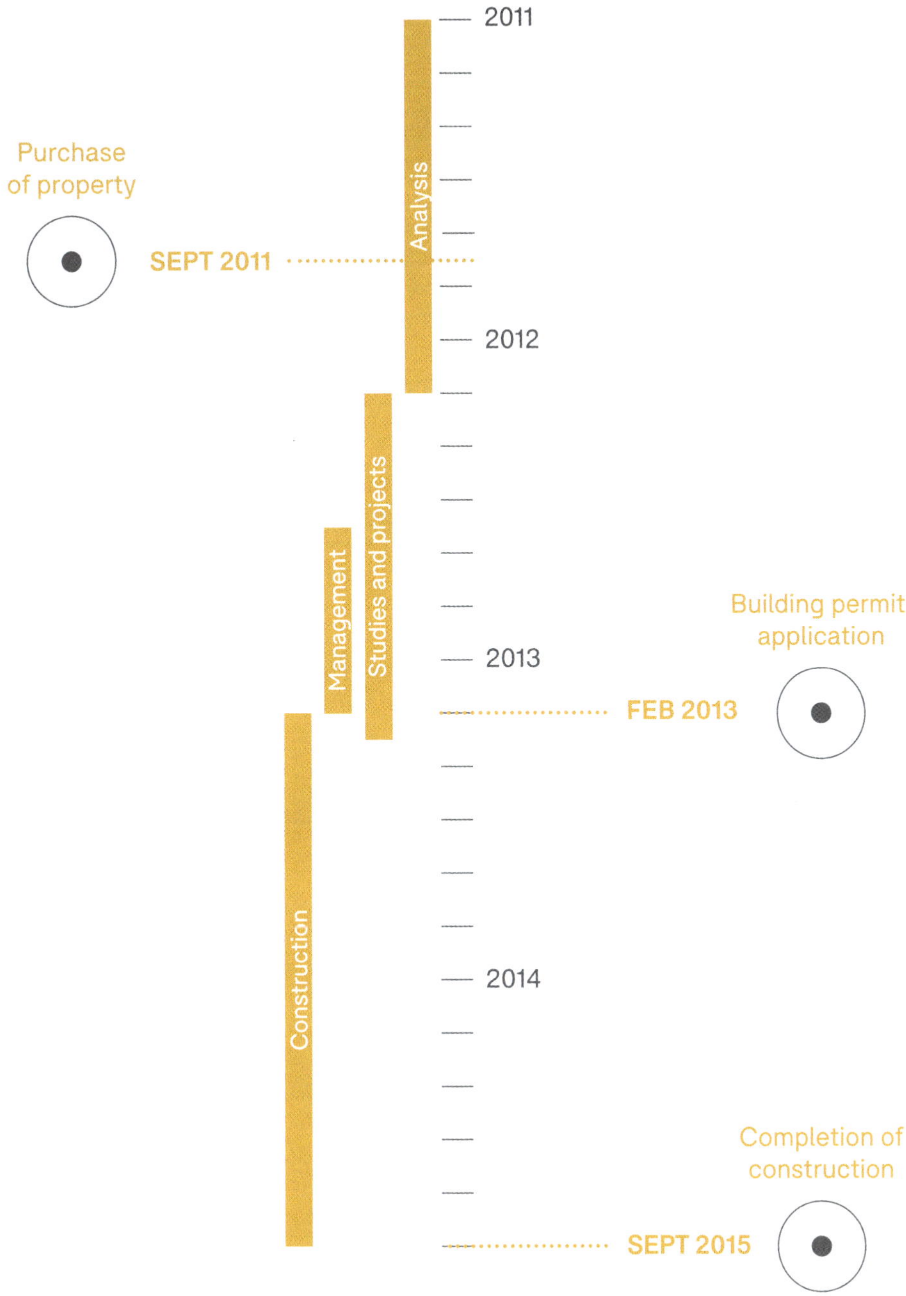
2011
Purchase of property
SEPT 2011
Analysis
2012
Studies and projects
Management
Building permit application
2013
FEB 2013
Construction
2014
Completion of construction
SEPT 2015

# Emilio Castelar 22

Location
Emilio Castelar 22
Colonia Polanco

Distance to public space
230 meters,
Parque Lincoln

Distance to public transport station
400 meters,
M Auditorio

Parking spaces
0

Year
2009 - 2011

Heritage list
INBAL

Record of previous uses
Residential

Current use
Commercial + residential

Percentage / $m^2$ recovered
100% / 1,530 $m^2$

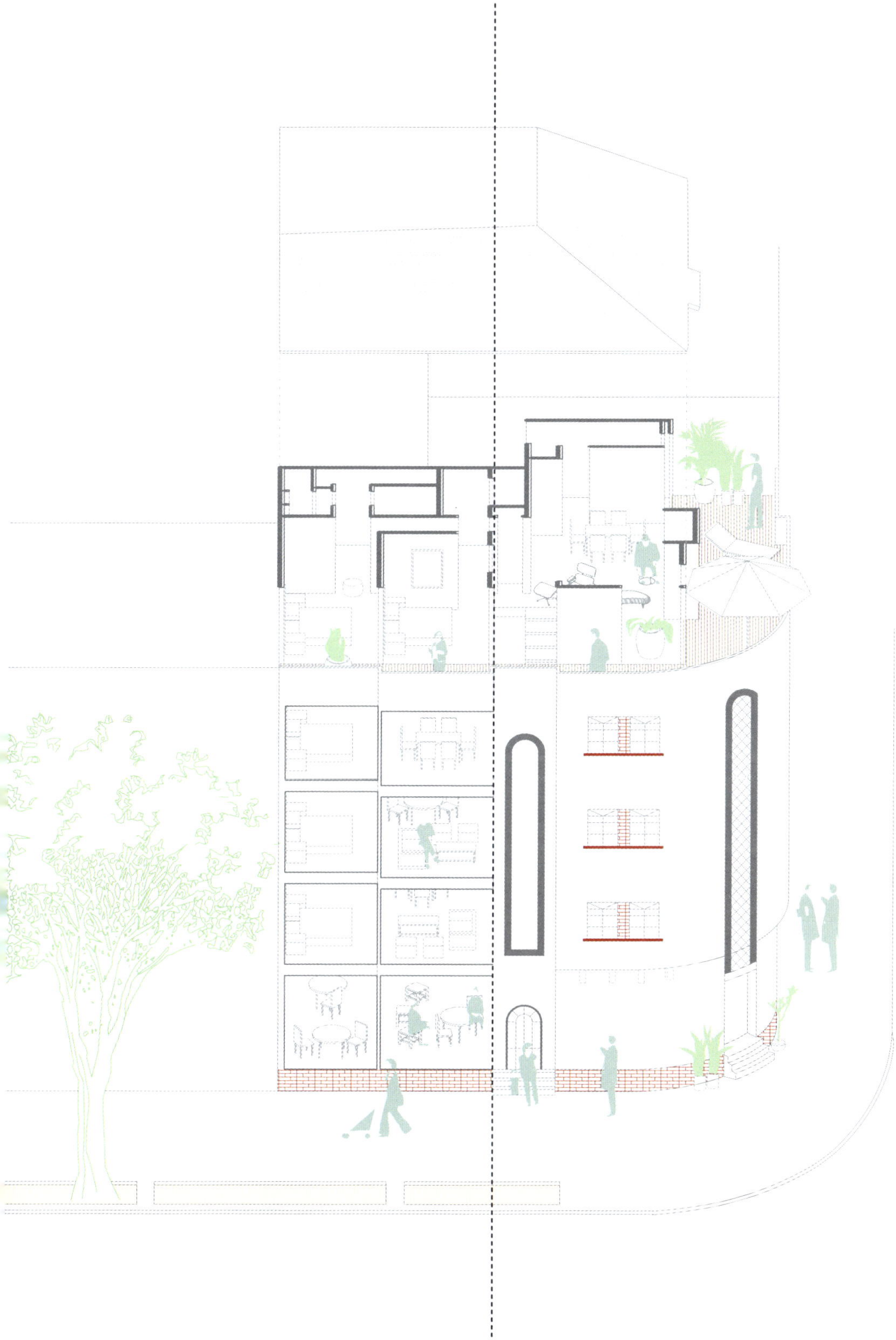

During the planning process with the local government authorities, it transpired that a law existed that exempted listed buildings of architectural heritage from the requirement to include parking spaces (prior to the regulatory change published in the Official Gazette in 2017). The building, Emilio Castelar 22, was just one block from Lincoln Park, in one of the most sought-after locations in the city. Aware that the property was in a dilapidated state, the aim was to add two apartments on the top floor of the building. However, the former parking regulation prevented this because it required a minimum of one parking space per apartment.

From that point on, and given that 40% of a building's cost goes toward foundations and parking, ReUrbano decided to work on rescuing buildings of significant heritage value.

---

## RESULT AND IMPACT

This project breathed life into the formerly desolate Calle Temistocles by creating a ground floor that opened onto the street with stores. The aim was to create many jobs and exterior public spaces where local residents and users could interact.

The impact of Emilio Castelar explains why we founded ReUrbano. We work with respect for heritage in order to preserve and improve the historic character of the neighborhoods where we intervene in order to propose a conscious and differentiated urban development model.

## LEARNINGS

We had the opportunity to discover a business niche in the recycling and reactivation of buildings in Mexico City, investing at the start of the global financial crisis, in October 2018. Whereas most developers were not interested in rescuing listed buildings, we saw a chance to avoid wasting square meters on cars.

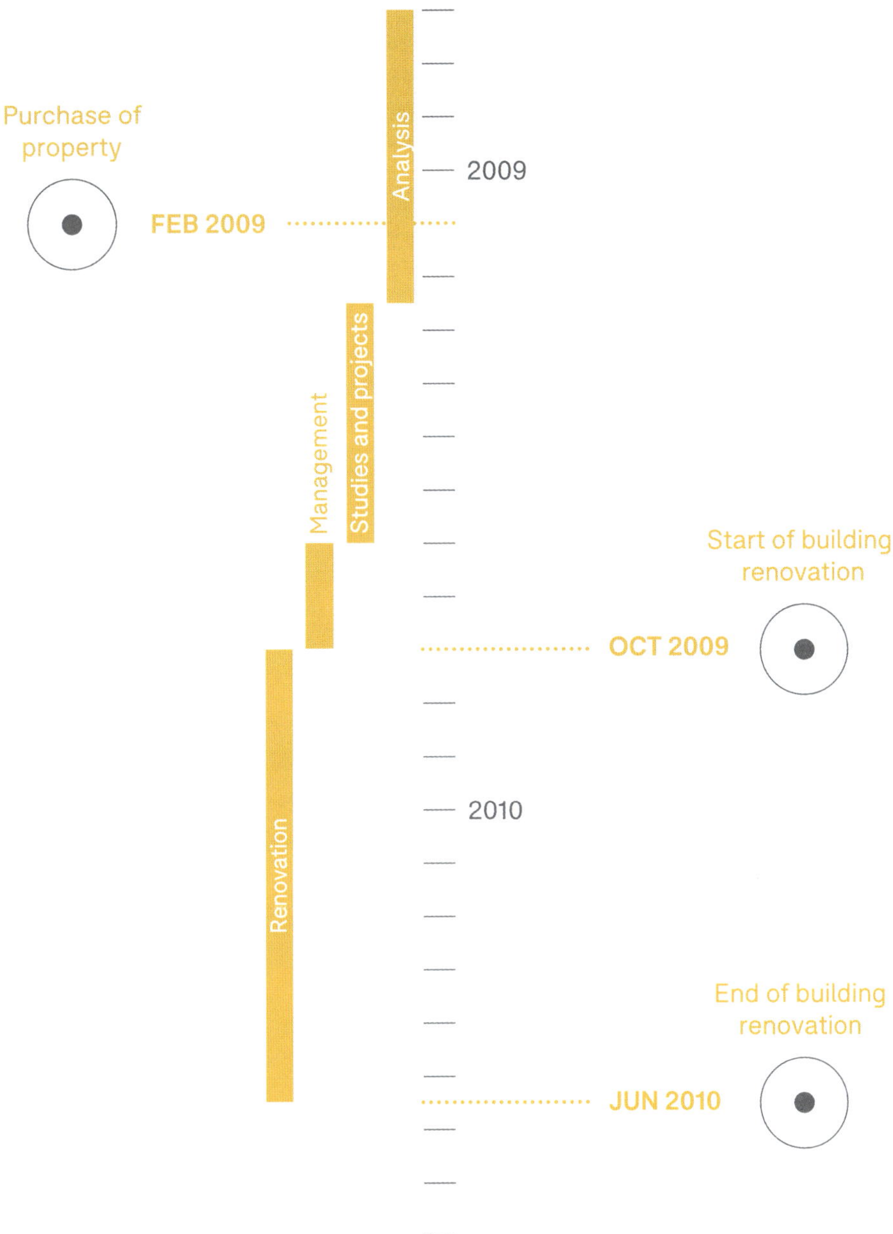
Purchase of property
FEB 2009
Analysis
2009
Studies and projects
Management
Start of building renovation
OCT 2009
Renovation
2010
End of building renovation
JUN 2010

SE RENTA
DEPARTAMENTO

HYATT REGENCY

THE
FEATHERED

THE
FEATHERED

# Emilio Dondé 7

**Location**
Emilio Dondé 7
Colonia Centro

**Distance to public space**
200 meters,
Plaza del Danzón

**Distance to public transport station**
250 meters, Ecobici

**Parking spaces**
0

**Year**
2018 - 2021

**Heritage list**
INBAL, INAH

**Record of previous uses**
Stationery store

**Current use**
Commercial + residential

**Percentage / $m^2$ recovered**
100% / 2,195 $m^2$

**Partner architect**
Juan Carral

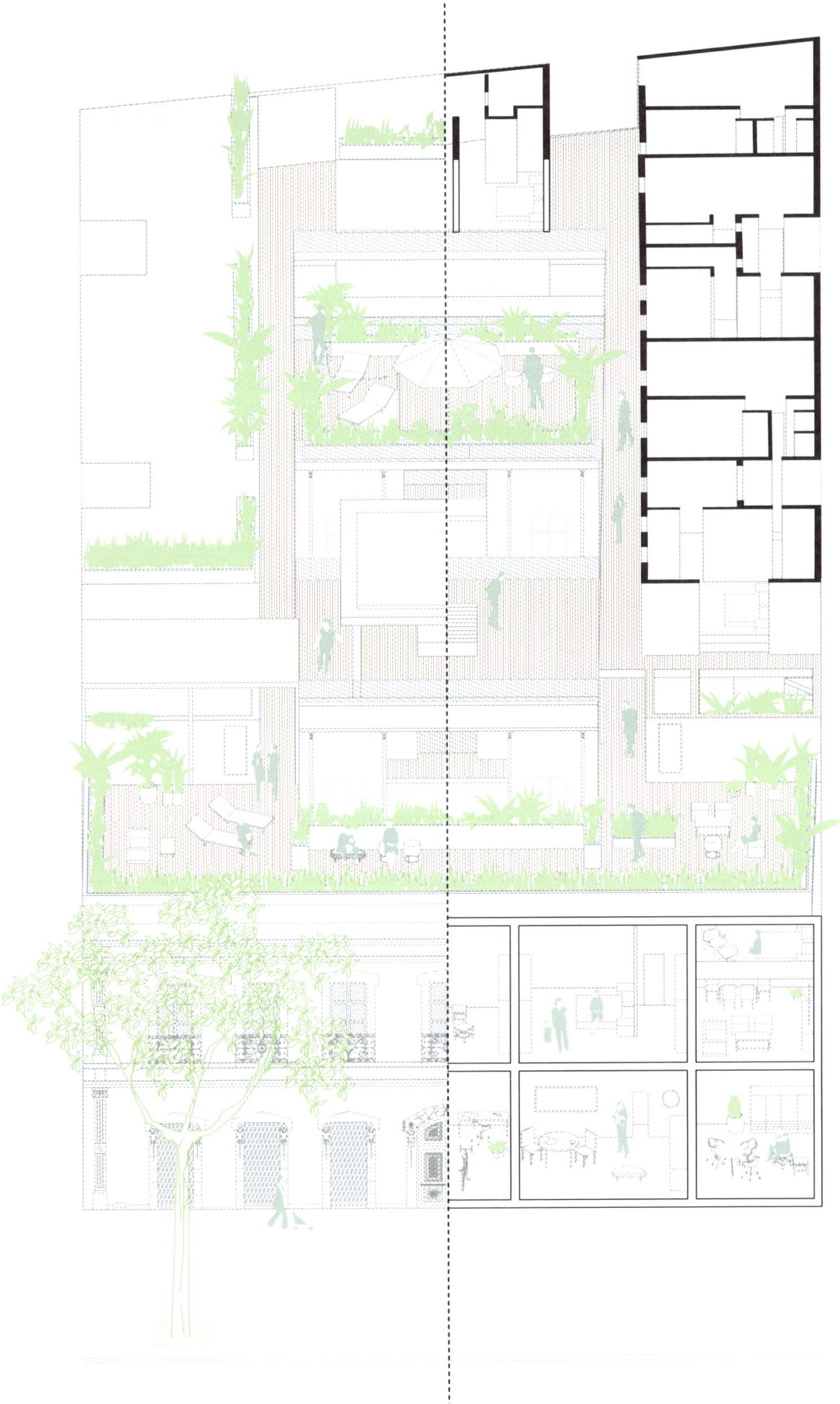

We need to work to rescue what we already have. You cannot make historic centers; they exist and our job is to look after them and activate them. Flexibility makes for the best housing, where something is always happening in the buildings. Heritage buildings are valuable because we no longer build in the same way as we did hundreds of years ago, and finding a contemporary means of inhabiting them is an important way of keeping a city's history alive in our minds.

We must create mixed cities and this requires a dialogue with government authorities, changing regulations to increase density and land use. The greater our understanding of buildings and people, the safer we will feel on the sidewalks; the areas in question will become more welcoming, and it will be more fun to live in the city. Whatever its location, a mixed-use building will be in use at all hours and a community will develop around it.

The intervention at Casa Emilio Dondé 7 is so subtle as to be almost imperceptible. The important aspect is the residential area and how it works. The building's base is solid, while the upper levels are more slender and lightweight. On the whole it is a well-designed structure.

---

## RESULT AND IMPACT

The project makes a positive impact on the city because of the potential for interventions on various buildings within a demarcated zone to create corridors. With various buildings along the same corridor, we can invest more in infrastructure such as sidewalks and planters.

## LEARNINGS

We have realized the benefit of collaborating with other developers where the partners handle most of the work, allowing us to focus on the project's actual design.

The opportunity lies in what we can learn from this process for future collaborations in order to avoid conflicts at the execution stage.

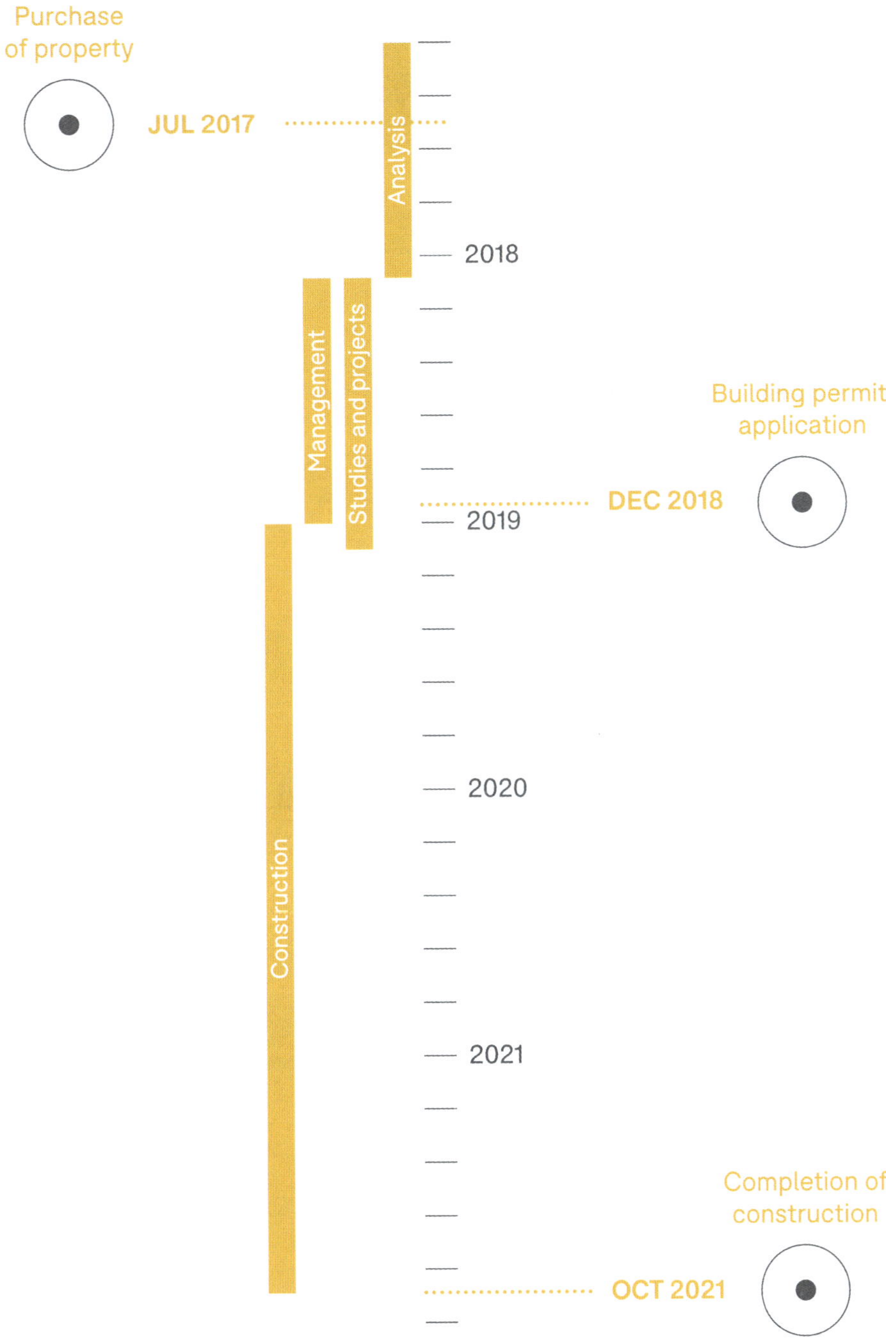
Purchase
of property
JUL 2017
Analysis
2018
Management
Studies and projects
Building permit
application
DEC 2018
2019
Construction
2020
2021
Completion of
construction
OCT 2021

# Emilio Dondé 68

Location
Emilio Dondé 68
Colonia Centro

Distance to public space
200 meters,
Plaza del Danzón

Distance to public transport station
450 meters,
MB Juárez

Parking spaces
42

Year
2015 - 2022

Record of previous uses
Auto repair
Diner
Hardware store

Current use
Commercial + residential

Partner architect
Cadaval & Solà-Morales

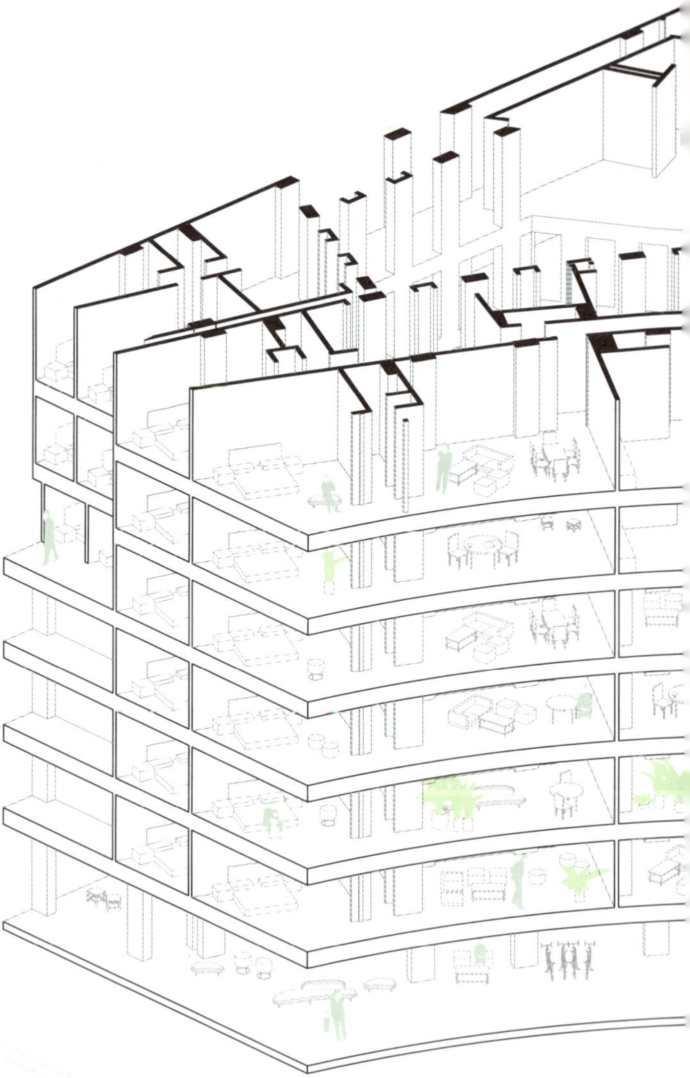

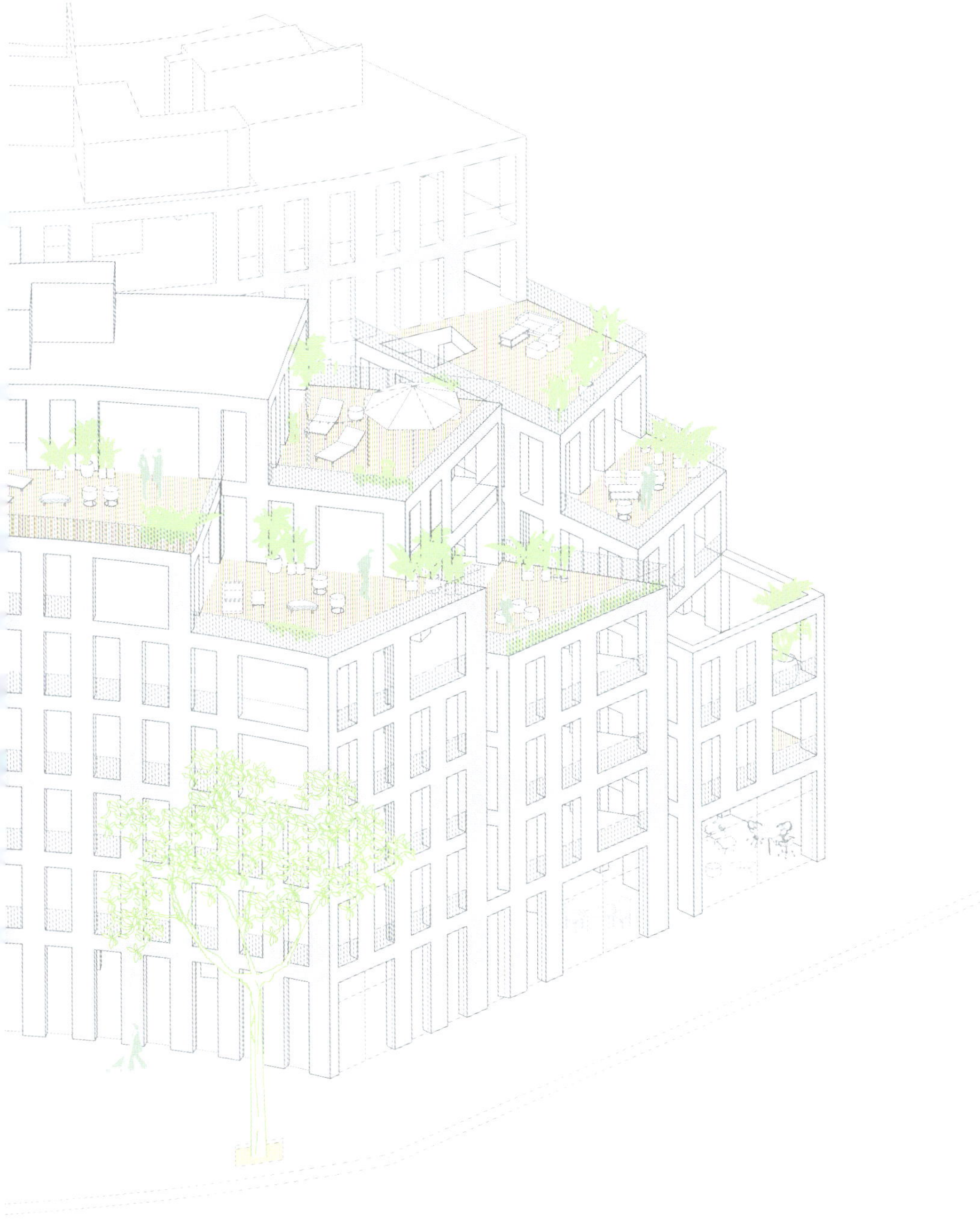

Dondé 68 is located on the iconic Bucareli avenue. This development incorporates the nearby Reloj Chino—a clock tower of significant historical and heritage value. ED68 seeks to provide an enclosure giving residents the best possible living conditions. Our strategy was to make it possible for people to appropriate the specially designed, well lit and naturally ventilated spaces that offer the finest possible views and a comfortable and cozy ambience.

This building has four volumes in total, joined by a central courtyard that brings natural light and ventilation into the building's residential areas. The geometry creates a building pared-down to its core essence, apparently straightforward but by no means simple. This simplicity adds strength to the solution, making it possible to achieve more with less. The terraces on the various levels provide views onto the Reloj Chino and the Plaza de la Ciudadela. The neighbors have been waiting for the area's reactivation, after a period of deterioration and abandonment, and this new vibrancy in the area will help attract new users.

## LEARNINGS

The flexibility in the design of the spaces has been essential in changing the original program as the project has progressed: during two phases, one large store became four smaller ones, and the number of residential units increased.

Keeping neighbors informed ahead of time helped minimize the inevitable sources of friction during a long and intense period of construction.

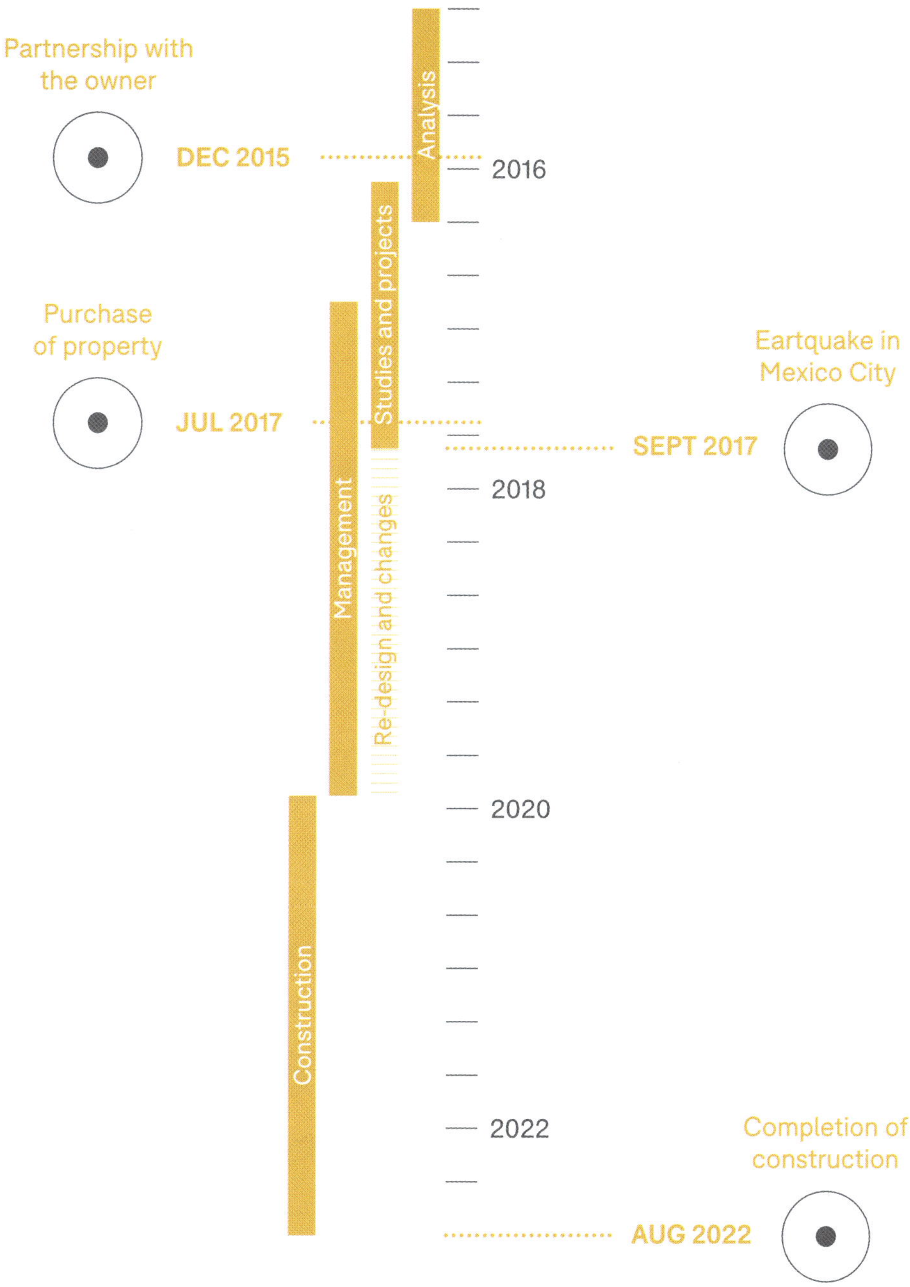
Partnership with the owner
DEC 2015
Analysis
2016
Studies and projects
Purchase of property
JUL 2017
Management
Eartquake in Mexico City
SEPT 2017
2018
Re-design and changes
2020
Construction
2022
Completion of construction
AUG 2022

# Havre 69

Location
Havre 69
Colonia Juárez

Distance to public space
600 meters,
Plaza Río de Janeiro

Distance to public transport station
260 meters,
MB Hamburgo

Parking spaces
0

Year
2011 - 2013

Heritage list
INBAL

Record of previous uses
Fonda San Diego

Current use
Commercial + residential

Percentage / $m^2$ recovered
100% / 534 $m^2$

Partner architect
Francisco Pardo
Julio Amezcua
(AT 103)

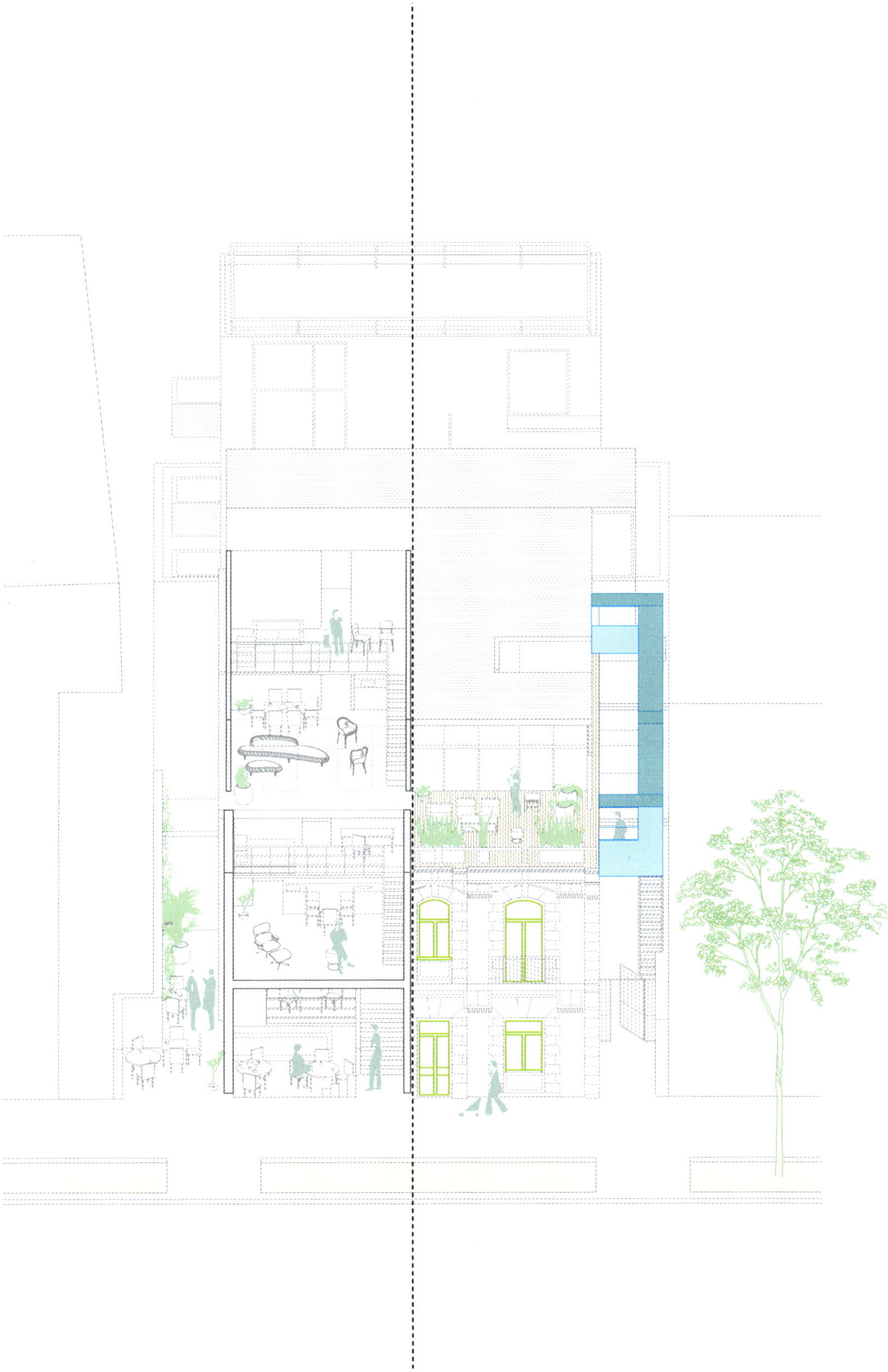

Originally, only four families lived at Havre 69. Our project has subdivided the former houses into 12 new residential units and a store: a bakery with the adjacent public space provides a link to the homes to create a mixed-use development attracting pedestrians to the area.

By creating new spaces to meet current needs, in a design that avoids the trap of faux historic buildings, this development uses, preserves, and consolidates architecture from the past and blends into its contemporary context.

Havre 69 sets up a new dialogue between the city, the neighborhood, and the former abandoned houses, at the same time as giving something back to its urban location by reactivating the area for the benefit of local residents. The project allows the city to penetrate it through narrow plazas on the side, and the bench opposite the store where pedestrians can take a rest, encouraging new urban relationships.

## RESULT AND IMPACT

Over and above the eagerness for novelty and to challenge the tastes of a sector of society, we can identify various responses to the need to redensify the city.

We support urban innovations (optimal use of space, sustainability, density). We also considered the market:

- Without becoming attached to a new product, in order to prioritize mixed-use developments
- Diversity of housing typologies and sizes
- Concentration of communal laundry areas
- Rescuing heritage blended with contemporary designs

## LEARNINGS

The lesson learned was to push harder for more investments along this corridor as opposed to starting to create other corridors from zero.

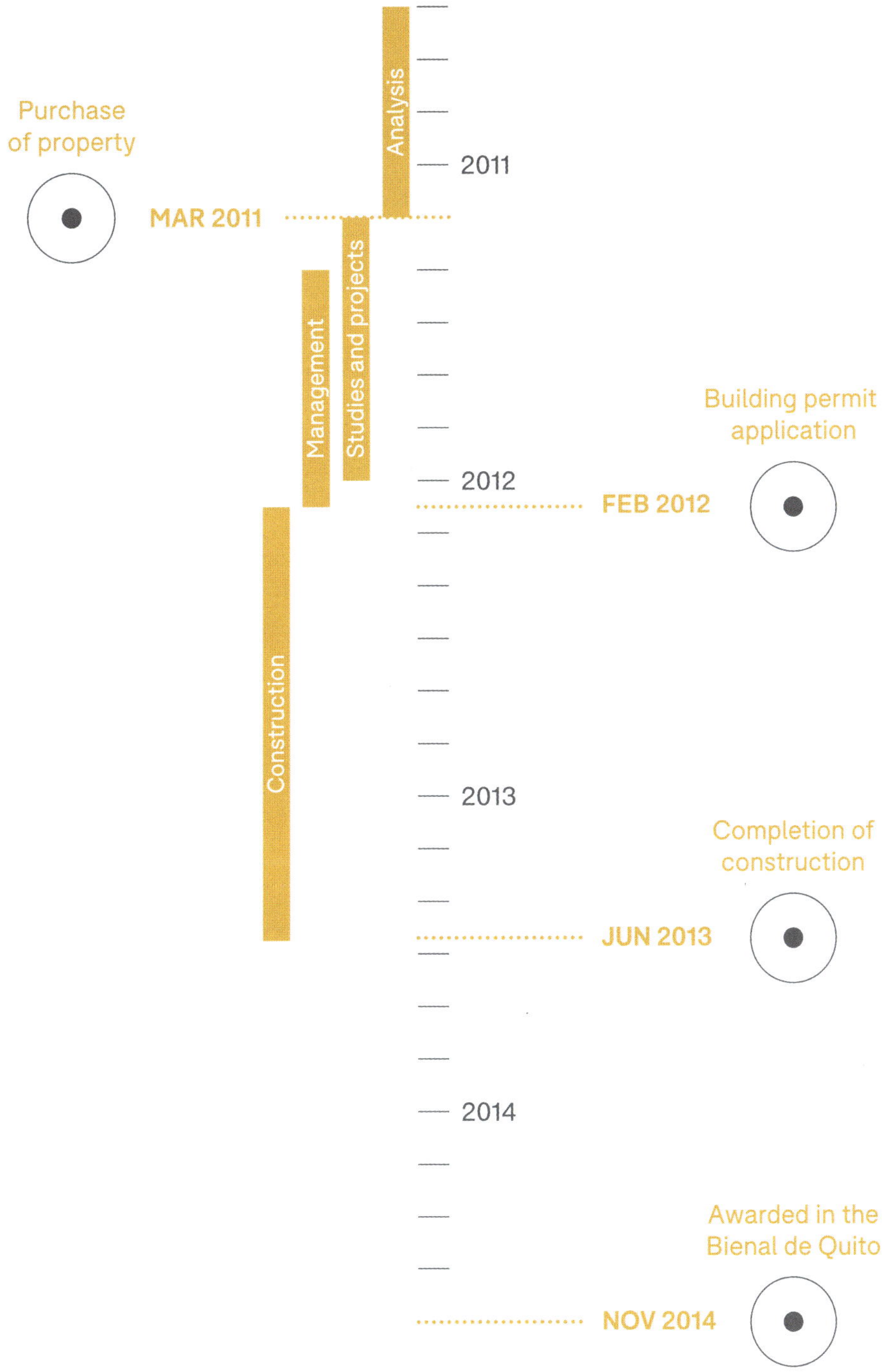
Analysis
2011
Purchase of property
MAR 2011
Studies and projects
Management
Building permit application
2012
FEB 2012
Construction
2013
Completion of construction
JUN 2013
2014
Awarded in the Bienal de Quito
NOV 2014

FONDA
SAN DIEGO

PANADERÍA
FONDA
SAN DIEGO

PANADERÍA
73

# Havre 77

Location
Havre 77
Colonia Juárez

Distance to public space
600 meters,
Plaza Río de Janeiro

Distance to public transport station
150 meters, Ecobici

Parking spaces
0

Year
2012 - 2015

Heritage list
INBAL

Record of previous uses
Vet
Perfumery

Current use
Commercial + residential

Percentage / $m^2$ recovered
100% / 320 $m^2$

Partner architect
Francisco Pardo
Julio Amezcua
(AT 103)

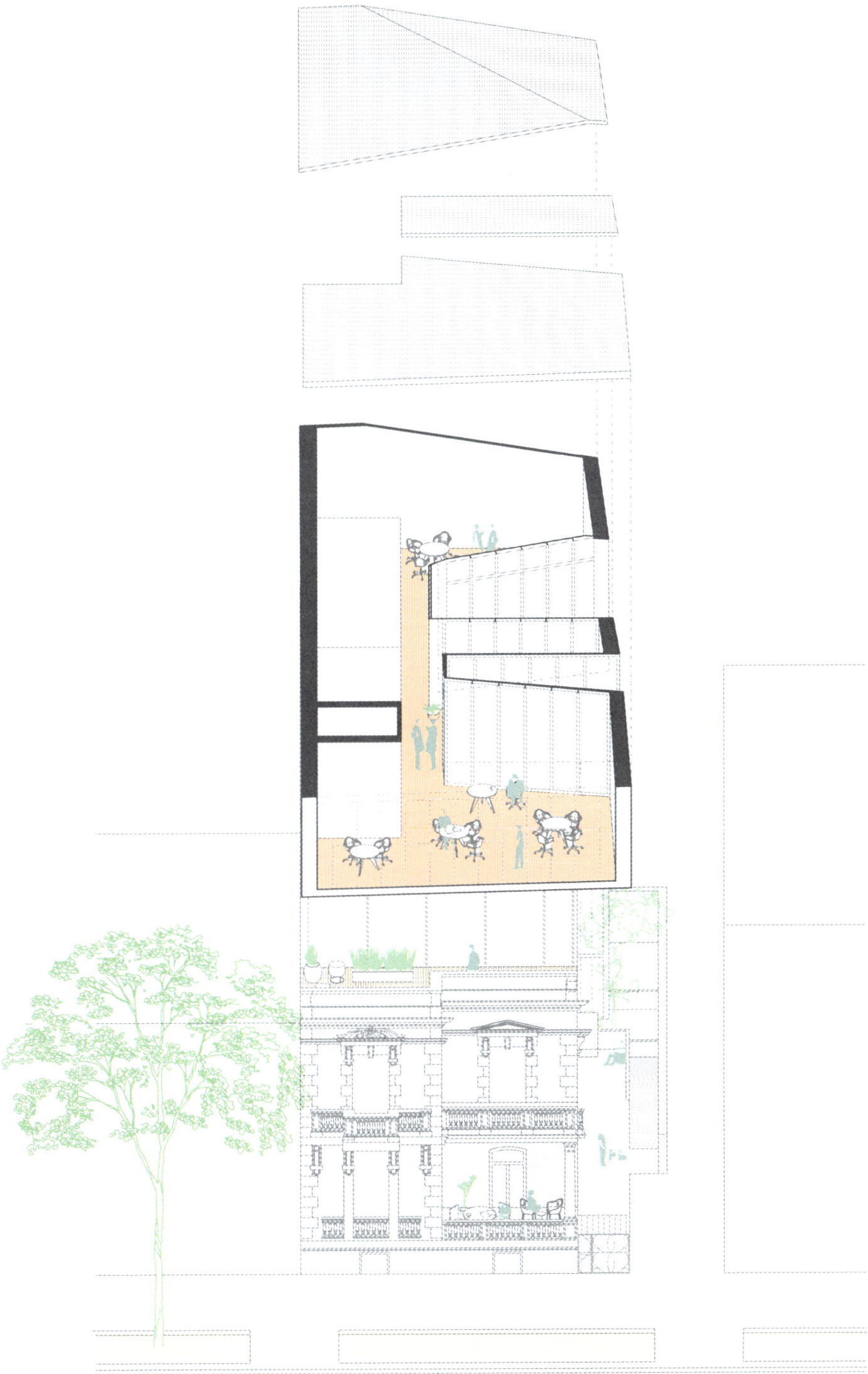

The responsibility and challenge of developing in a city that changes as much as Mexico City is not only about *demolishing* to *build*: it is about creating spaces that respect and understand their context. Harmonizing past and present to consolidate processes of urban regeneration through authentic and differentiated projects.

The Havre 77 development was designed as a mixed-use space with restaurants on the ground floor and offices on the other levels. This strategy has successfully created 24-hour activities between Havre 77 and Havre 69. Upon completion of the project, in collaboration with La Lonja Mx (a traveling market that promotes and assembles the best Mexican designers and producers), ReUrbano applied for a permit to close three blocks along Havre (from Calle Liverpool to Avenida Chapultepec) to set up market stalls in the public space.

## RESULT AND IMPACT

A single development was achieved in two buildings through the right balance of mixed-usages. Havre 77 came after Havre 69, but it is the most well-calibrated combination after sales of residential projects had already begun along the corridor. It was the obvious next step to add another project to offer more street life while the new residents are working.

## LEARNINGS

The effects of the initial investments could already be felt in the buzzing activity on the street, in the urban trends (reappraising the neighborhood), and so it was understood that we could benefit most by entering the area as soon as possible.

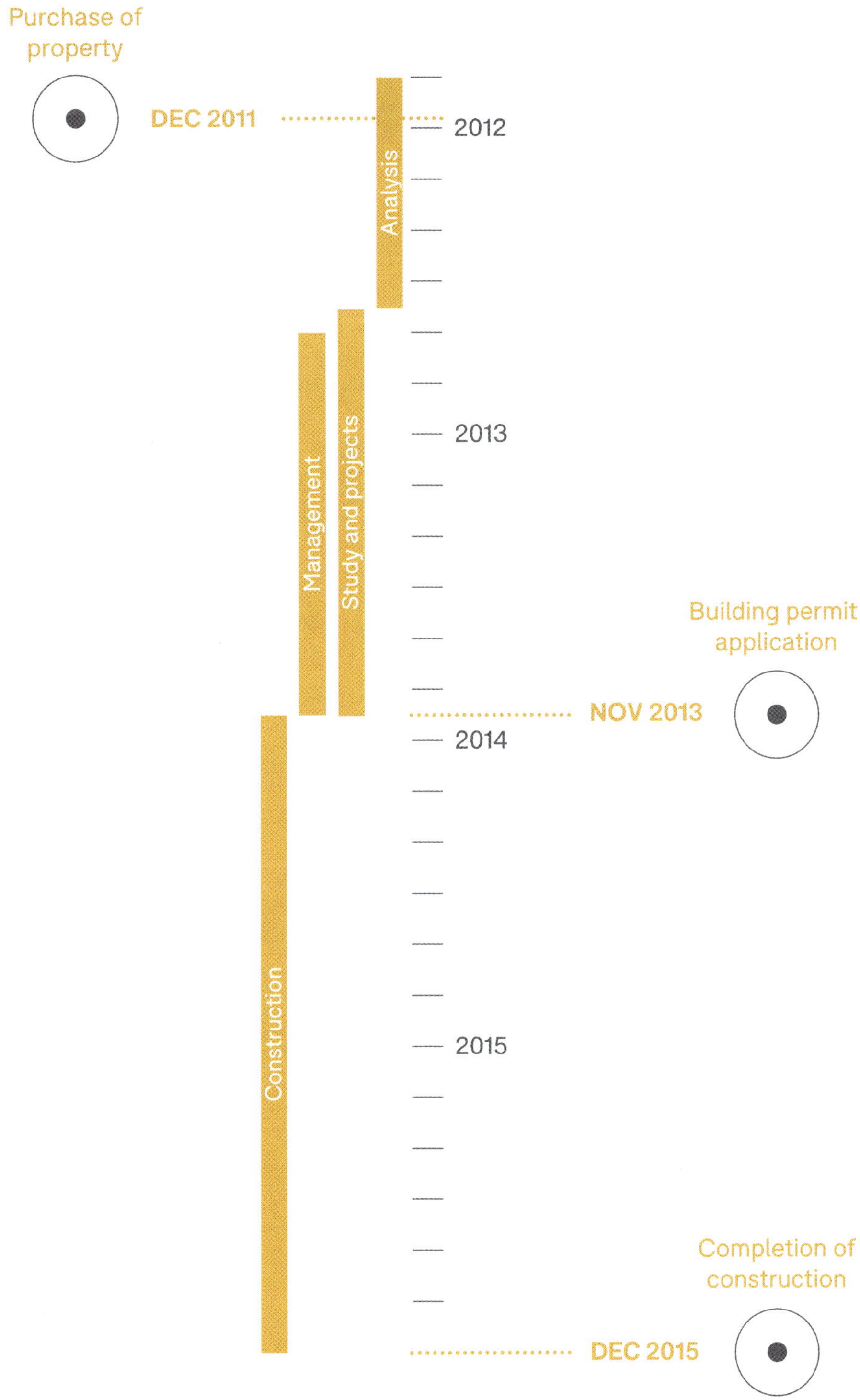
Purchase of property
DEC 2011
2012
Analysis
2013
Management
Study and projects
Building permit application
NOV 2013
2014
Construction
2015
Completion of construction
DEC 2015

H77

# Havre 83

Location
Havre 83
Colonia Juárez

Distance to public space
550 meters,
Plaza Río de Janeiro

Distance to public transport station
350 meters,
MB Hamburgo

Parking spaces
0

Year
2012 - 2015

Heritage list
INBAL

Record of previous uses
Residential

Current use
Commercial +
Oficinas

Percentage / $m^2$ recovered
100% / 320 $m^2$

Partner architect
Juan Segura

When ReUrbano acquired Havre 83, a "for sale" sign had been hanging from Juan Segura's building for more than two years. Since then, it has become a seed for new businesses and growth. ReUrbano's first offices were on Calle Havre, at a time when our firm had barely more than two partners and three employees. Today, our development company employs 40 people directly.

In parallel to ReUrbano, BUNA - Café Rico embarked on its own business venture. After establishing the brand, the business moved to new premises in the Roma while maintaining its coffee-production center in the Doctores neighborhood. In this way Havre 83 has helped activate and develop successful microbusinesses.

---

## RESULT AND IMPACT

This was our first attempt at adapting a building by adding a pre-existing commercial premises to the new project.

## LEARNINGS

Havre 83 marked a watershed in the initial projects of Mexico City's real-estate boom, to replicate a highly leveraged investment model by working with investors.

This project merged various elements: ReUrbano's low profile and lack of competition. Subsequently, similar renovation and refurbishment projects were carried out. These circumstances made it possible to buy a complete building at a good price and with a rapid execution.

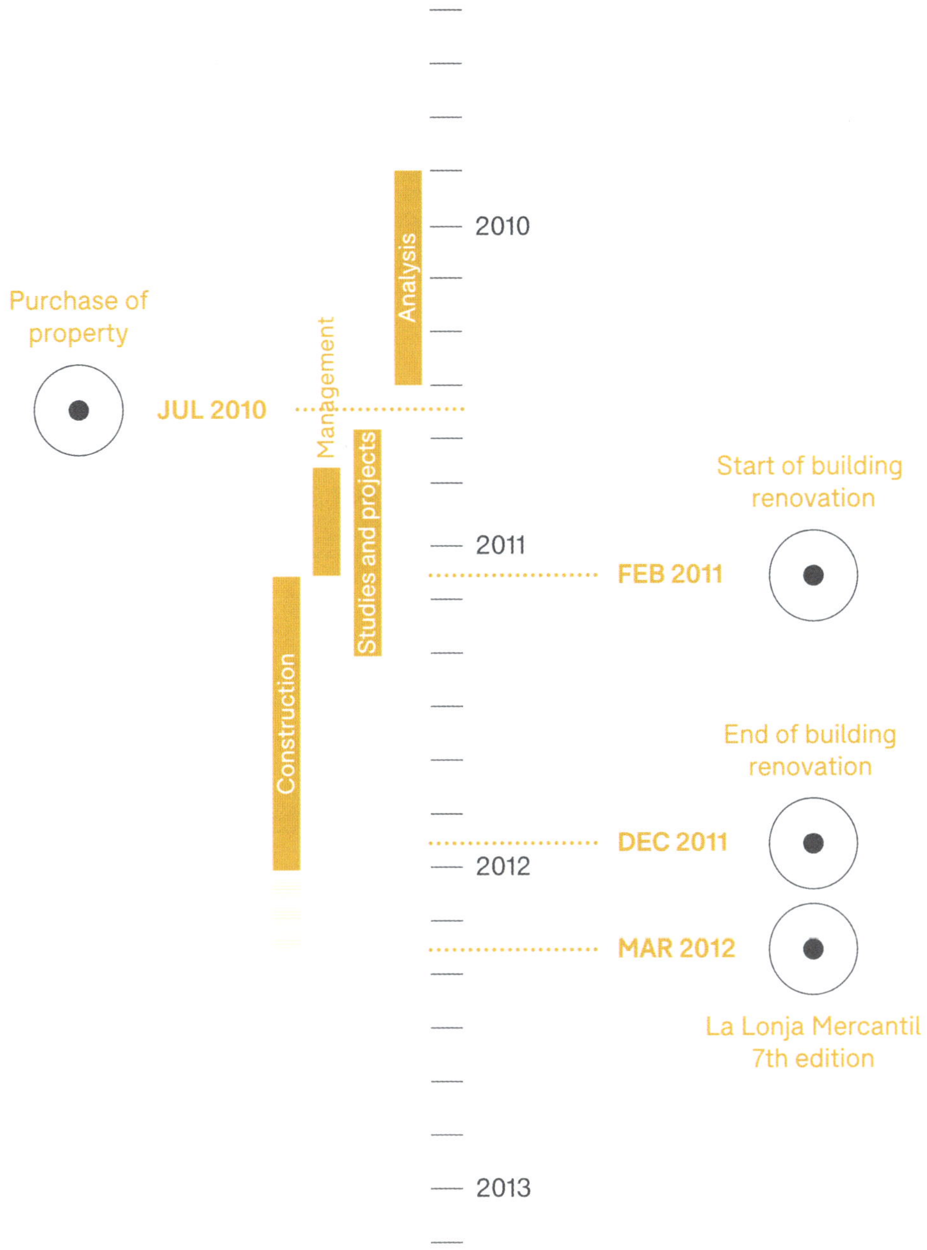
2010
2011
2012
2013
Analysis
Management
Studies and projects
Construction
Purchase of property
JUL 2010
Start of building renovation
FEB 2011
End of building renovation
DEC 2011
MAR 2012
La Lonja Mercantil 7th edition

# Iztaccíhuatl 54

Location
Iztaccíhuatl 54
Colonia Condesa

Distance to public space
50 meters,
Parque México

Distance to public transport station
400 meters,
MB Campeche

Parking spaces
0

Year
2015 - 2017

Heritage list
INBAL

Record of previous uses
Residential

Current use
Commercial +
Short-term accommodation

Percentage / $m^2$ recovered
100% / 1,240 $m^2$

Partner architect
La Metropolitana

ReUrbano began a participative process to explain to local residents how a project that integrated business premises would not only improve the existing urban appearance.

In Iztaccíhuatl 54 it was necessary to alter the pre-existing façade. The idea was to turn the windows into doors in order to optimize the practicality of the ground-floor businesses; by maximizing the connection between the business and the street we could effectively adapt and integrate the project within its context. With this in mind, we lodged an application with the INBA—Mexico's government institute in charge of listed buildings—to modify the façade, detailing our rationale in various letters. After several attempts, the INBA conditioned their approval for the modification on the agreement of the neighbors, who supported the idea of low-impact businesses (no bars, nightclubs, or valet parking) that involved the community. At the end, we received the green light to go ahead with the program.

---

## RESULT AND IMPACT

We have maintained a good relationship with the neighbors, we respect the opening hours, and the street is now buzzing with activity.

The project's low-impact and correct understanding of the regulatory instruments created a successful heritage, business, and tourist project.

## LEARNINGS

This heritage project forms part of an investment vehicle that does not recognize this model and as a result, since the development concluded maintaining it in the portfolio has proven costly.

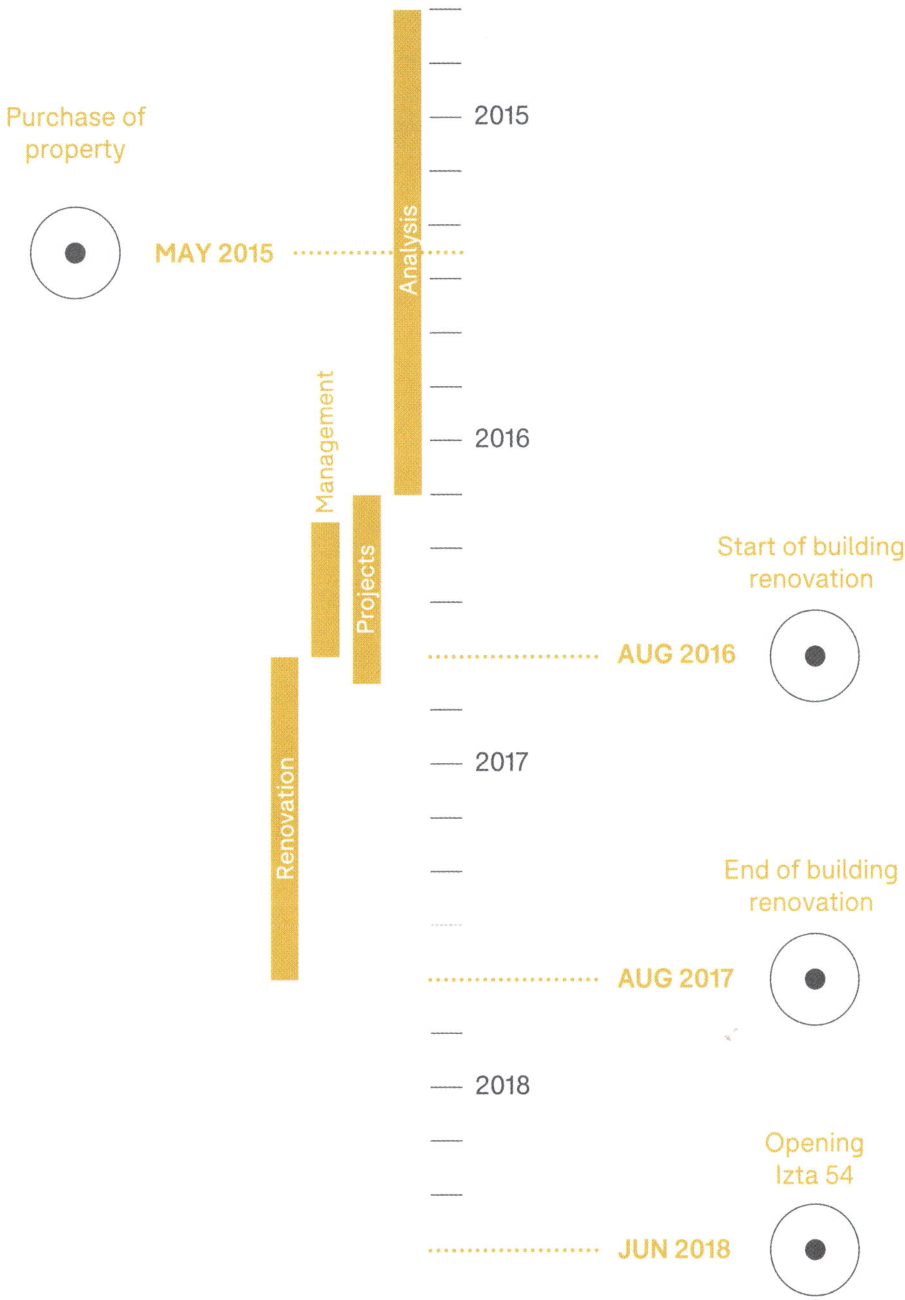
Purchase of property
MAY 2015
2015
Analysis
2016
Management
Projects
Start of building renovation
AUG 2016
Renovation
2017
End of building renovation
AUG 2017
2018
Opening Izta 54
JUN 2018

CHAI YÓ
THE WAY OF TEA
EDIFICIº
SAN FERNANDOº
54

EDIFICIº
SAN FERNANDOº

IZTA 54

# La Laguna

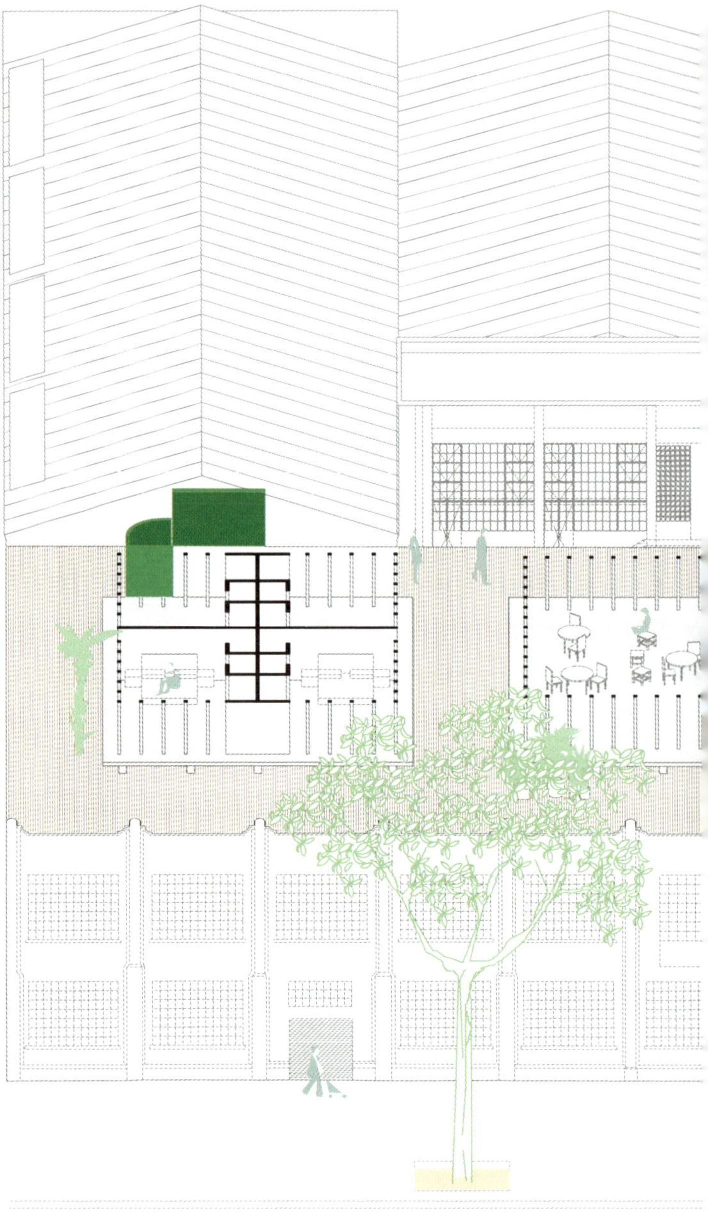

Location
Dr. Erazo 176
Colonia Doctores

Distance to public space
280 meters,
Jardín Pushkin

Distance to public transport station
250 meters,
MB Jardín Pushkin

Parking spaces
0

Year
2017 - Under construction

Heritage list
INBAL

Record of previous uses
La Laguna, S.A.
Spinning and bannisters factory

Current use
Workshops + Offices

Percentage / $m^2$ recovered
100% / 6,455 $m^2$

Partner architect
La Metropolitana

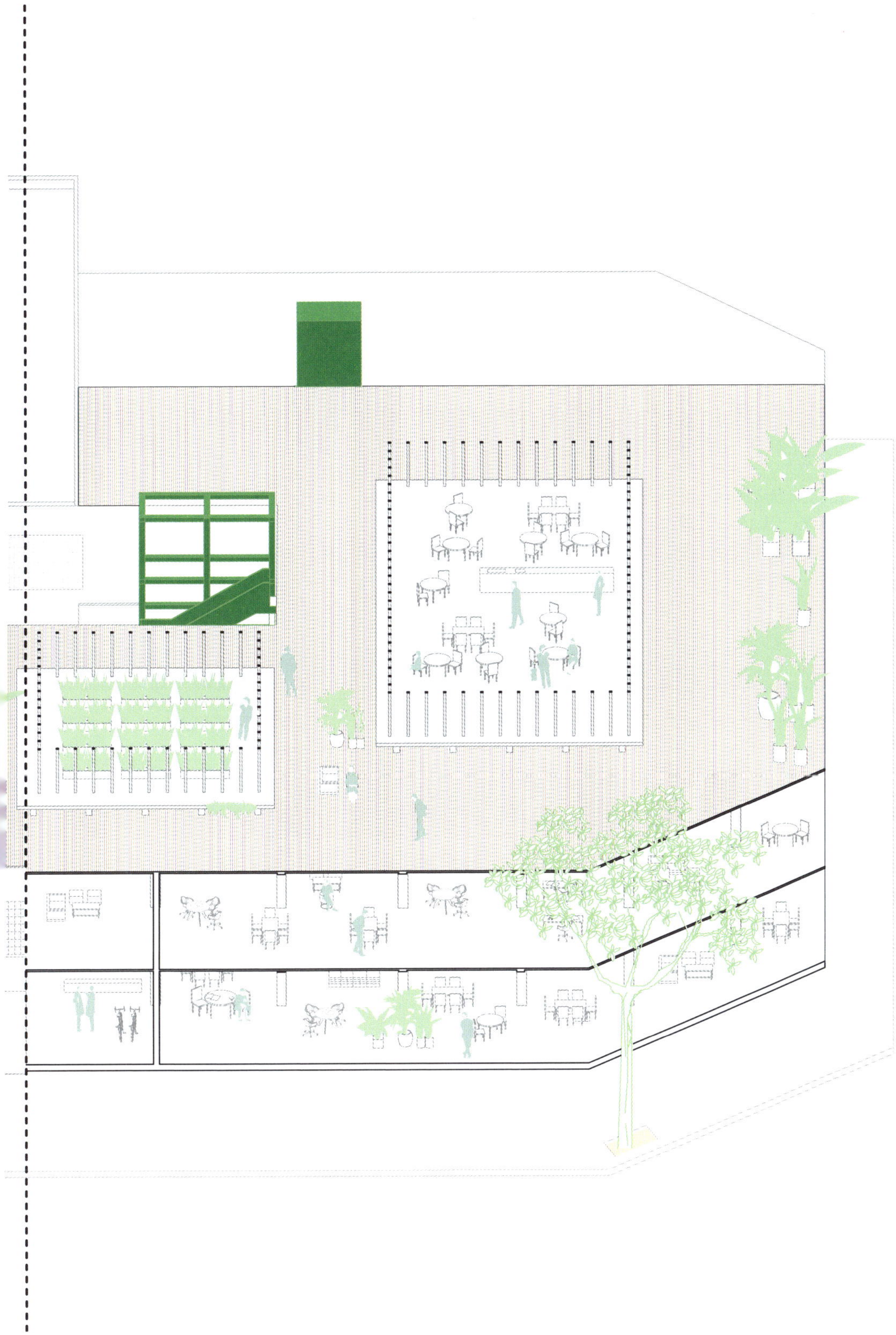

Preserving a city's built heritage is not simply about aesthetics: old buildings tell stories and inform citizens about a past that they could not witness. For those who reject such cultural romanticism, another reason exists to avoid demolishing our cities' old buildings: humanity is dangerously close to exhausting Earth's resources, and we must begin to question our predilection for the new. Normally the term "recycling" refers to the use of disposable plastics, paper and cardboard boxes, but the time has come to apply it to unused buildings.

Some years ago, a textile and lace factory in the Doctores neighborhood closed after being in business for almost 100 years. The property—three floors around a central courtyard, an ironwork grid of large picture windows, a distinctive green façade—is as large as its potential. The first new tenant was BUNA, a Mexican coffee company that installed its roasting equipment inside the former factory. It was followed by design and architecture studios that saw the possibility for creating a community in the building, and thus La Laguna began to take shape as a complex of offices, workshops and spaces open to the public as a means of reactivating the area.

---

### RESULT AND IMPACT

Through its work, ReUrbano has formed a network of partners over the years so that they can become the initial users of an anchor-project for further investments in the area.

### LEARNINGS

A successful project is not enough to generate local opportunities. The role of land use from a heritage perspective becomes important when building a flexible project whose construction takes place in stages largely using the flows generated through a program of modular activation. In other words, the product or program effectively responds to the structure of capital and expectations of a return on investment.

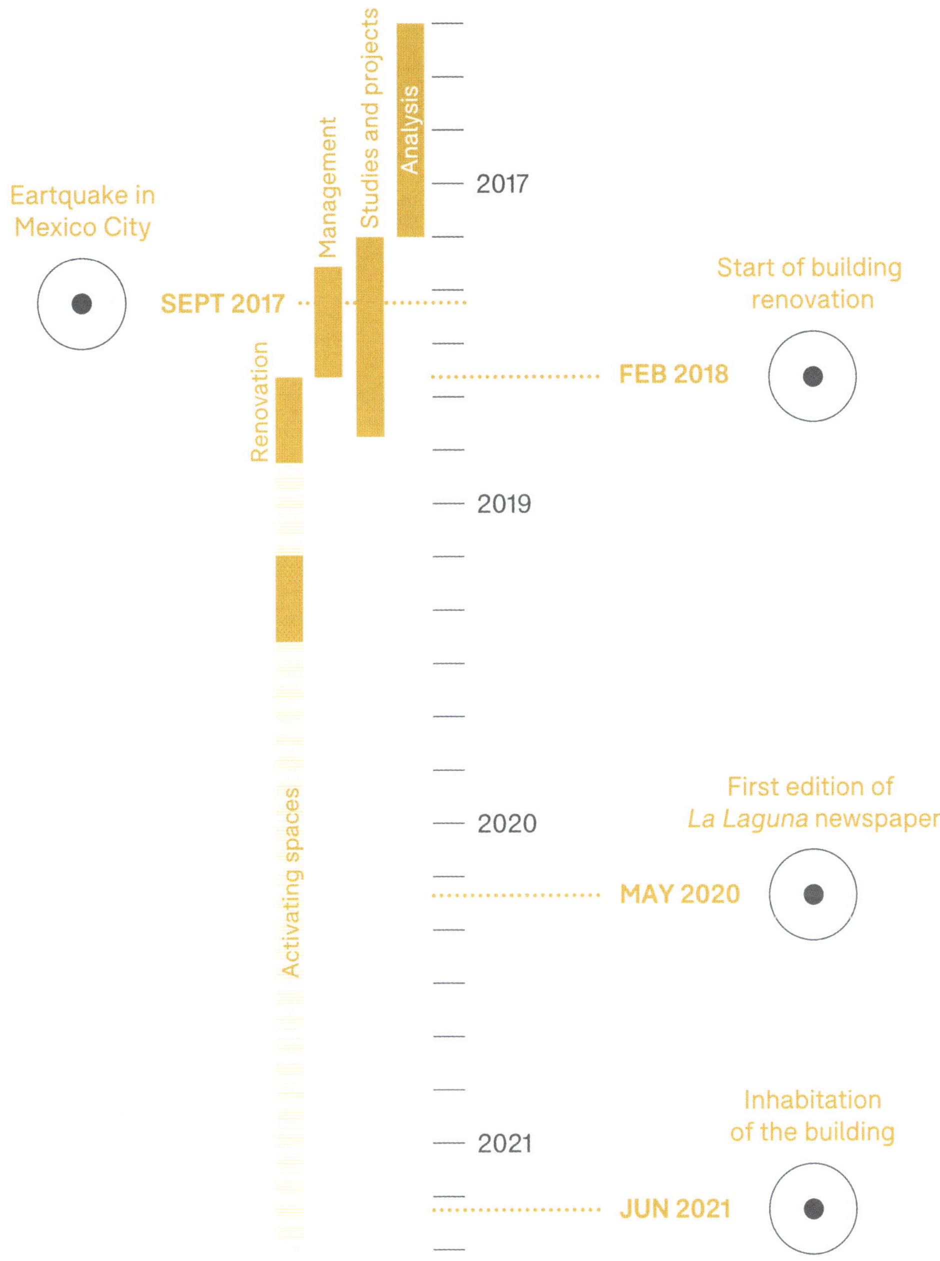
Eartquake in Mexico City
SEPT 2017
Start of building renovation
FEB 2018
First edition of *La Laguna* newspaper
MAY 2020
Inhabitation of the building
JUN 2021
Analysis
Studies and projects
Management
Renovation
Activating spaces
2017
2019
2020
2021

# Liverpool 9

Location
Liverpool 9
Colonia Juárez

Distance to public space
10 meters, Plaza Giordano Bruno

Distance to public transport station
250 meters, Ecobici

Parking spaces
0

Year
2013 - 2021

Heritage list
INBAL

Record of previous uses
Ice cream shop
Hairdressers
Stationers

Current use
Commercial + residential

Percentage / $m^2$ recovered
100% / 1,210 $m^2$

Partner architect
MMX

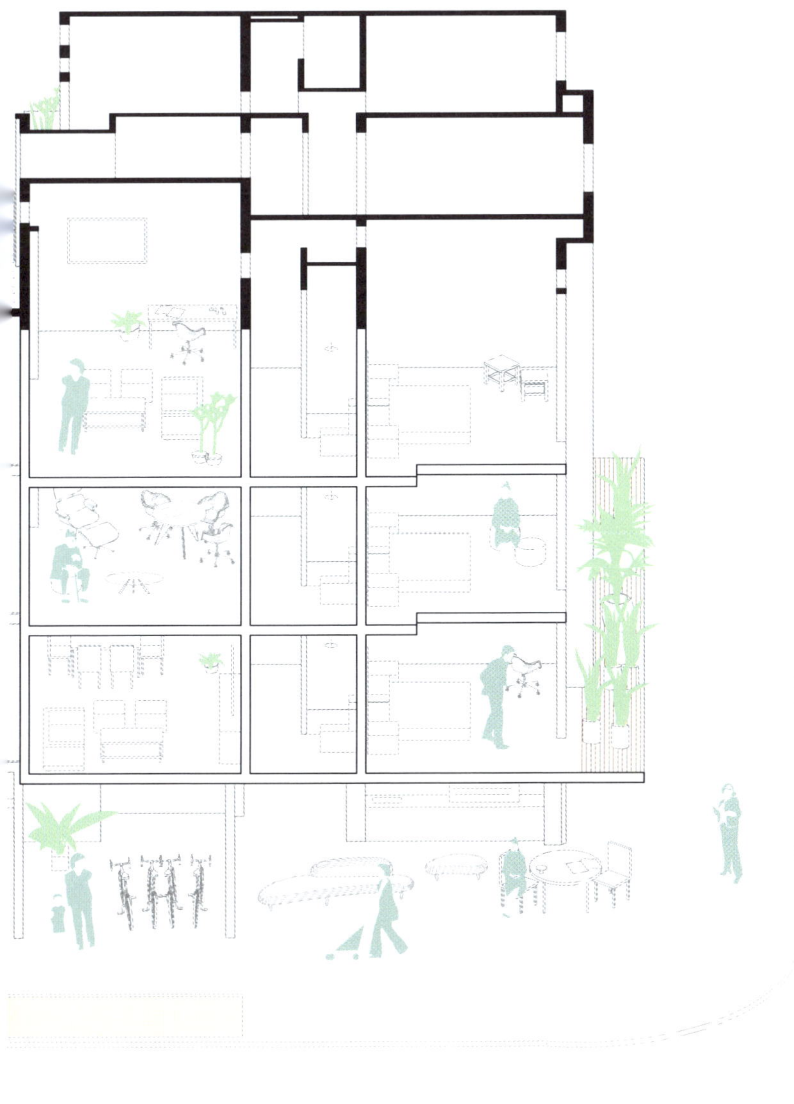

The Juárez neighborhood, like many neighborhoods near Reforma and the city center, is at the heart of the city and has undergone various periods in its varied history. We believe this area to be key to the central urban area because it connects downtown with areas to the west. Its greatest potential lies in this urban connection.

Liverpool 9 is a small development with only 10 residential units and ground-floor commercial premises. Pedestrianizing the city was important as it meets the needs of people looking for residences in well-connected areas without the need for cars because of the close proximity to public transport and all kinds of services. This lifestyle is nothing new to the Juárez neighborhood; therefore the recovery of this property is not only about rescuing a building but also preserving and intensifying the area's urban dynamics.

The project itself was straightforward. By focusing on rescuing the building in its original form, we did not change any finish anywhere on the façade and left the interiors largely unaltered. Each apartment continues to boast period moldings and features, an important factor because those living in this building should be aware of its rich history.

## RESULT AND IMPACT

The development involved restoring the building from its deteriorated state while preserving the sense of the building's natural aging. The key lies in drawing attention to the historical value of the buildings themselves: keeping a piece of that history alive is important for a city.

## LEARNINGS

We learned about the importance of developing a close relationship with the community at the initial stages of the project with methodologies that combine the perspective of the various stakeholders interacting in cities with others building alternatives and solutions to real problems.

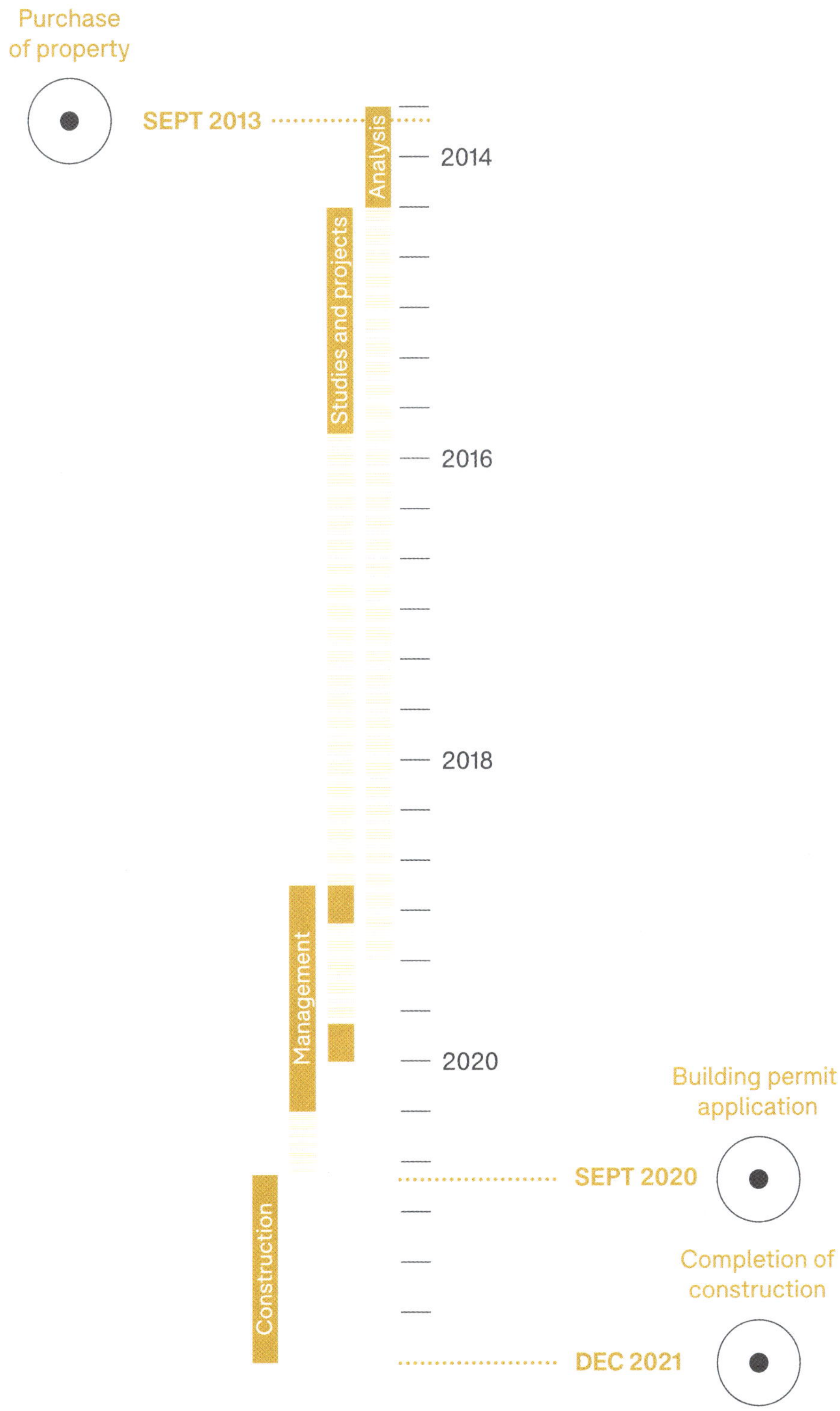
Purchase
of property
SEPT 2013
Analysis
2014
Studies and projects
2016
2018
Management
2020
Building permit
application
SEPT 2020
Construction
Completion of
construction
DEC 2021

Ensaladas

# Milán 44

Location
Milán 44
Colonia Juárez

Distance to public space
300 meters,
Plaza Giordano Bruno

Distance to public transport station
450 meters,
MB Reforma

Parking spaces
0

Year
2013 - 2016

Record of previous uses
Auto repair

Current use
Comercio + Oficina

Percentage / $m^2$ recovered
100% / 1,055 $m^2$

Partner architect
Francisco Pardo
Julio Amezcua
(AT103)

The context of this development obliged us to apply a different criteria than when evaluating the pre-established values of listed or heritage buildings. We believe that the history or style of pre-existing constructions are not the sole reason they form part of the local area; these buildings are intrinsically valuable for the neighborhood.

The decision to preserve the entire structure of a former four-story warehouse defines Milán 44. The pre-existing auto parts shop's façade was completely blind to the street. ReUrbano chose to respect the pre-existing structures regardless of whether or not they were listed by the authorities, based on the idea that preserving the structure and opening up the opaque façade would give the building a new public purpose. This openness would also provide a sense of safety to benefit the area, in line with Jane Jacobs' principle of "eyes on the street."

At the street level, apart from a restaurant, the development aims to open up the building as a public space that is vibrant during the whole day, in order to invite the community to join in its varied activities.

## RESULT AND IMPACT

The success and lessons learned from this project are based on the space's flexibility: Milán street has had three different lives in the few years since our work was completed, and it could even have more. A market, yoga space, events venue, offices, restaurants, and so on. It could even be reconverted into a housing development.

## LEARNINGS

Each project has a high-impact interconnection with its neighborhood, with public space and with the city. The occupation of public space by marginal groups has brought all kinds of contrasts. It teaches us that even with the execution of a large and efficiently designed project, there will always be a level of uncertainty in this area.

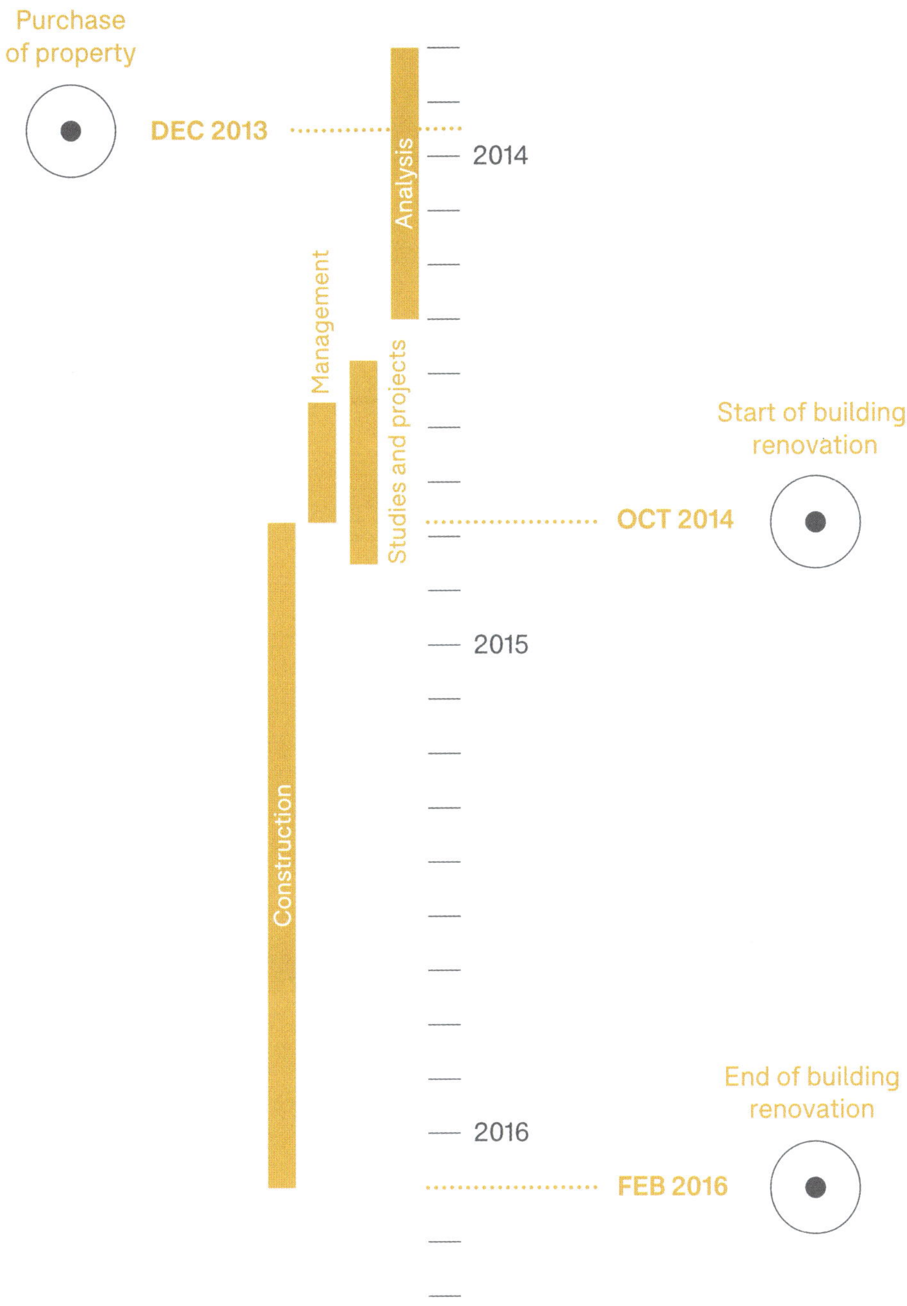
Purchase of property
DEC 2013
2014
Analysis
Management
Studies and projects
Start of building renovation
OCT 2014
2015
Construction
End of building renovation
2016
FEB 2016

CASSO
AUTO ELECTRICA CASSO, S.A. DE C.V.
PARTES ELECTRICAS
PARA:

MILÁN 44

MILÁN 44

2.

MILÁN 44

# Manuel Dublán 46

Location
Manuel Dublán 46
Colonia Tacubaya

Distance to public space
800 meters,
Parque Lira

Distance to public transport station
350 meters,
M Tacubaya

Parking spaces
0

Year
2015 - 2020

Heritage list
INAH

Record of previous uses
Single-family dwelling

Current use
Commercial + residential

Percentage / $m^2$ recovered
100% / 565 $m^2$

Partner architect
PRODUCTORA

Manuel Dublán is an apartment building with a ground-floor store built within and on top of an early-20th-century courtyard house. The pre-existing, two-story construction was completely renovated, restored, and reused as a home with high ceilings; some units included tapanco loft spaces. The new building's layout is centered on the original courtyard, where the preservation of the pre-existing tree helps the building's internal micro-ecosystem, offering privacy, temperature, and shade.

The new levels added over the historic façade, toward the interior, create an urban scale that is friendly for pedestrians and establishes a respectful dialogue between the original building and the new addition, creating large, sheltered terraces.

Interconnecting the upper stories, a new sculptural staircase floats over the central courtyard and has the same blue color as found in the details of the original house. The apartments on the upper stories take advantage of the circulation spaces to create private, open-air outdoor areas. The two upper stories now contain duplex apartments with direct access to the rooftop terraces with 360-degree panoramic views over the city.

---

## LEARNINGS

The Manuel Dublán 46 development's building permission process posed a challenge: it took 34 months to arrange the paperwork for a 17-apartment project. Tacubaya has a long history and significant potential to become one of the best areas in which to live and visit the city. However, the area's regeneration has taken longer than expected. Pre-sales were made at a very early stage, at very low prices (even below the unit cost of production). As a result, this combination of factors pushed the desired price higher than planned.

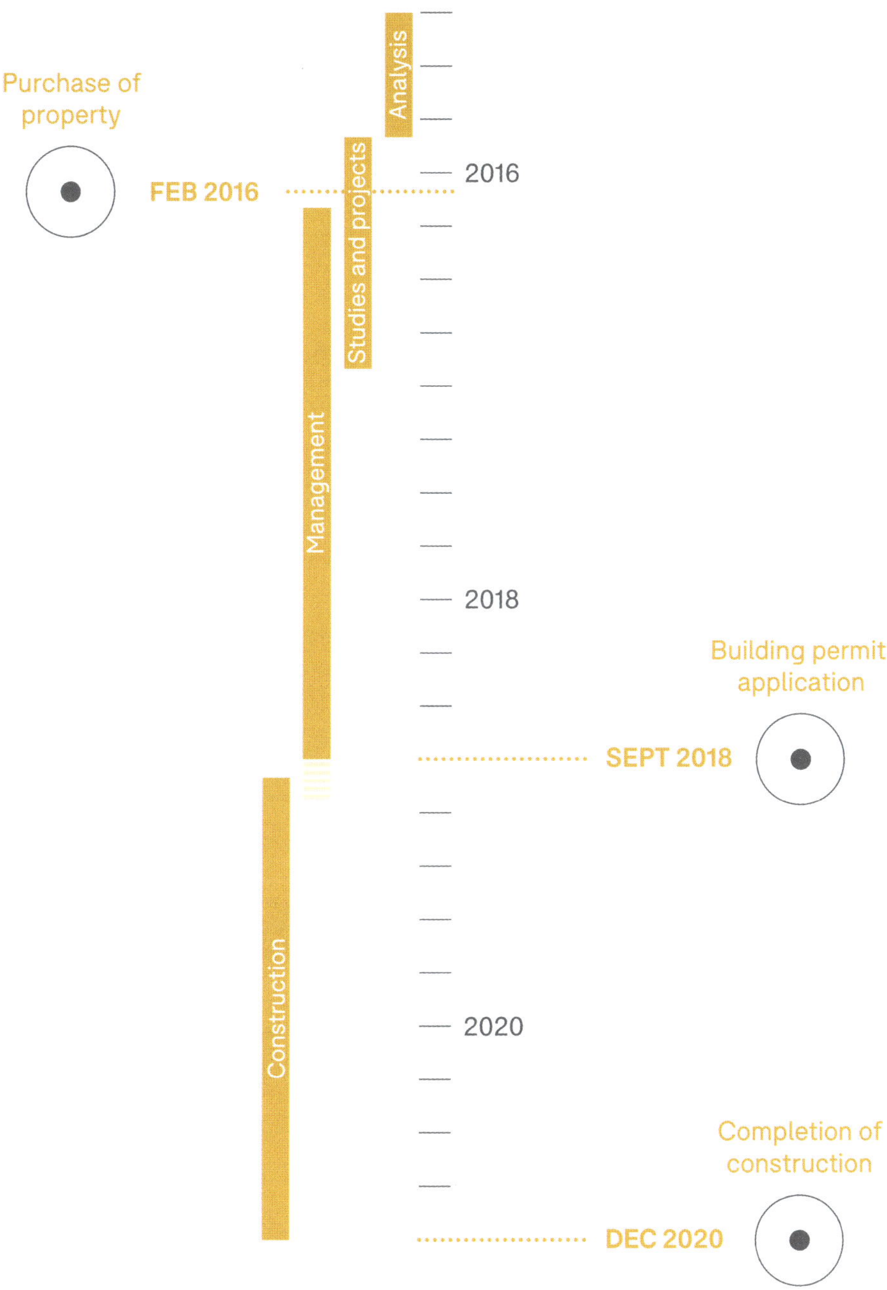
Analysis
Studies and projects
Management
Construction
Purchase of property
FEB 2016
2016
2018
Building permit application
SEPT 2018
2020
Completion of construction
DEC 2020

# Sindicalismo 76

**Location**
Sindicalismo 76
Colonia Escandón

**Distance to public space**
500 meters,
Jardín Morelos

**Distance to public transport station**
500 meters,
MB Nuevo León

**Parking spaces**
0

**Year**
2017 - 2021

**Record of previous uses**
Dry cleaners

**Current use**
Commercial + residential

**Percentage / m² recovered**
100% / 1,240 m²

**Partner architect**
Francisco Pardo

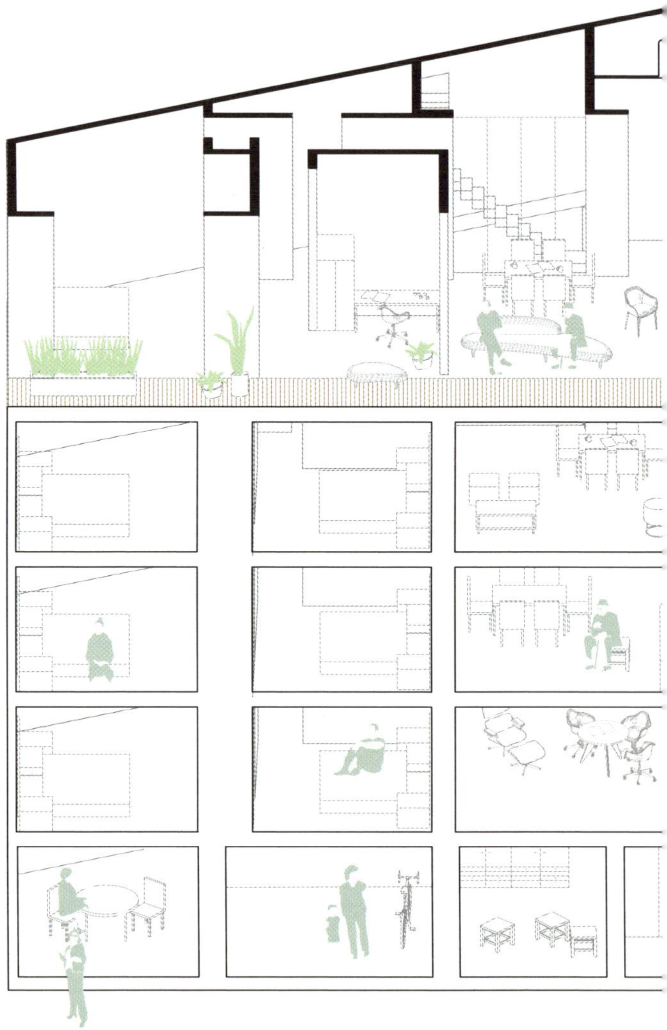

The Escandón is one of Mexico City's most iconic neighborhoods, with a vibrant street life, a thriving art and gastronomic scene, as well as eclectic architecture with examples of art deco and functionalist styles.

Sindicalismo 76 is a renovation and remodeling project on a construction built in 1955. The intervention respects the building's original layout, while taking advantage of the existing built area without increasing density, improving the quality of some inhabitable spaces. For example, the interior apartments open up onto the courtyard to create a terrace.

The building's façade has elements representative of the functionalist style found in many of the buildings dating from the 1950s in Mexico City. With its muted color palette, the façade has ironwork window frames painted black, with decorative stone features, a red ceramic-tile cladding and black-painted ironwork.

---

### RESULT AND IMPACT

Regulations change. If we were to decide to build the 1955 project today the current zoning laws and use of land would make it illegal. Many interventions on existing buildings fall into this category, hence the importance of the building's history (previous licenses) as the basis for deciding on the number of apartments and mixed uses.

### LEARNINGS

We learned that pre-sales are a liability with (monetary and non-monetary) interest payable for every day delivery is delayed.

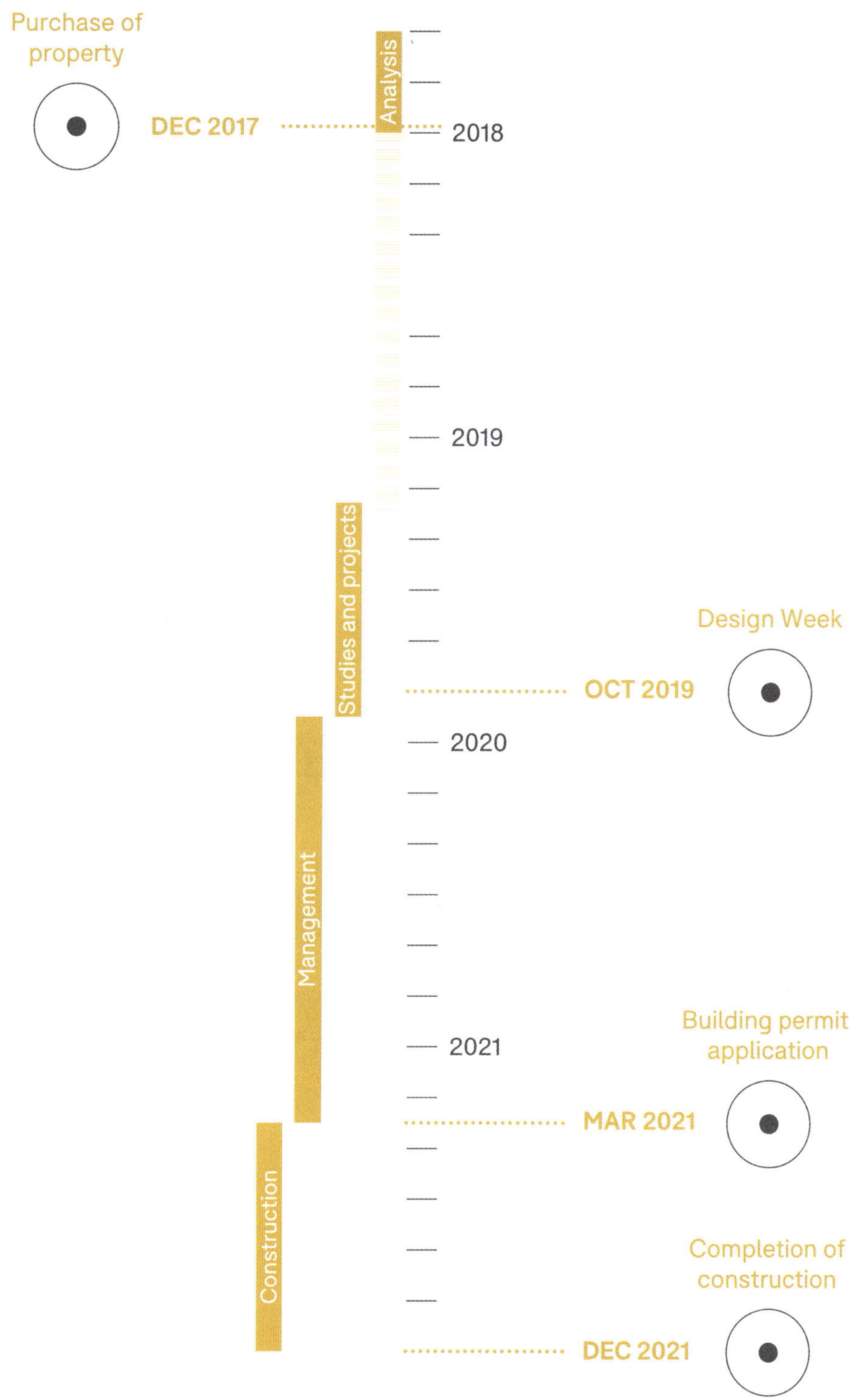
Purchase of property
DEC 2017
Analysis
2018
2019
Studies and projects
Design Week
OCT 2019
2020
Management
2021
Building permit application
MAR 2021
Construction
Completion of construction
DEC 2021

SINDICALISMO
SINDICALISMO

# Versalles 84

Location
Versalles 84
Colonia Juárez

Distance to public space
170 meters,
Plaza Giordano Bruno

Distance to public transport station
450 meters,
M Cuauhtémoc

Parking spaces
0

Year
2013 - Under construction

Heritage list
INBAL

Record of previous uses
Residential

Current use
Commercial + residential

Percentage / $m^2$ recovered
100% / 3,050 $m^2$

Partner architect
MMX

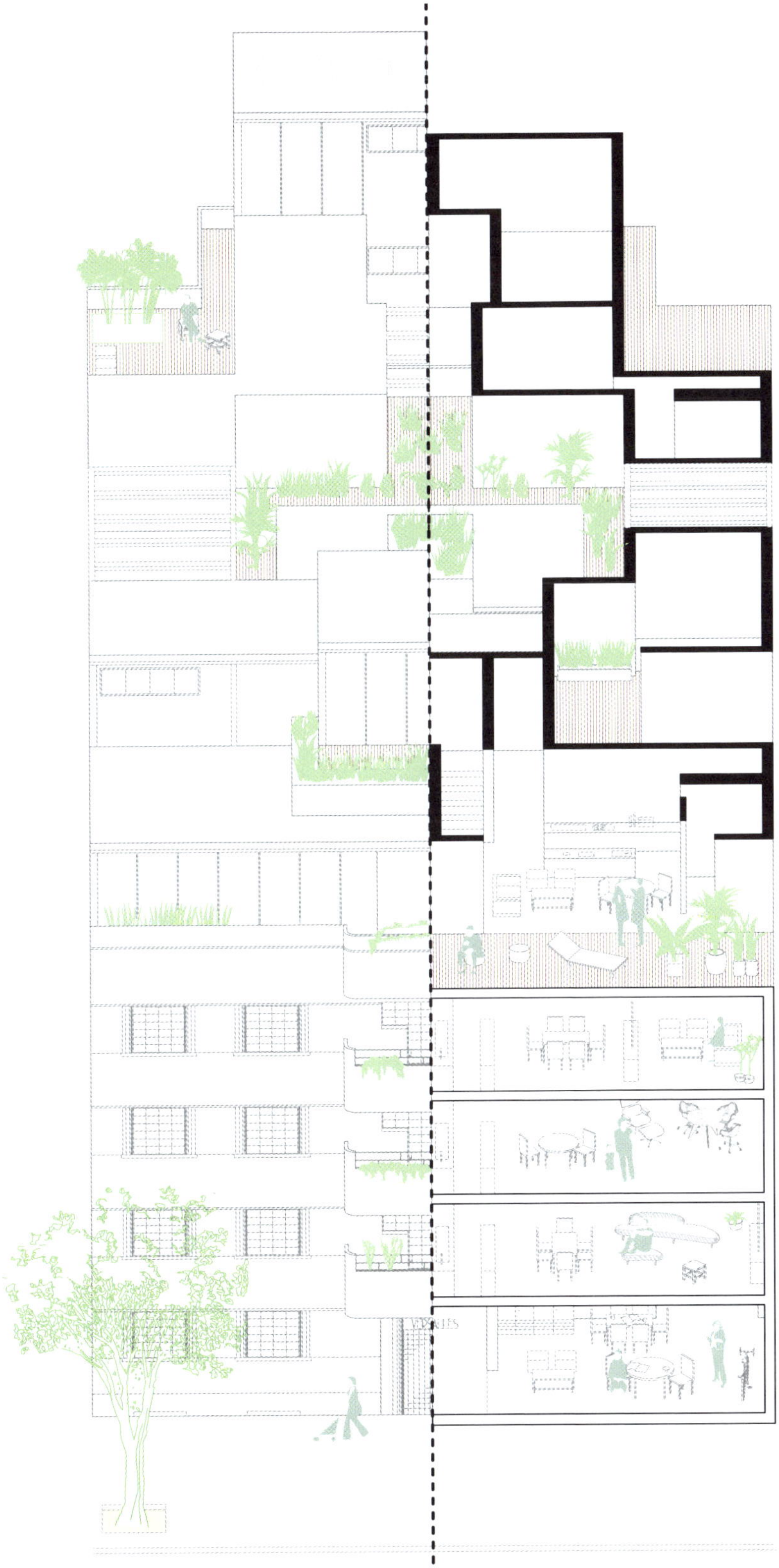

Mexico City grew rapidly during the 1920s and 30s with the creation of new lots and subdivisions. In some cases, the new constructions were built in the art deco style, and this gives a special feel to these streets.

Versalles 84 in the Juárez neighborhood is one example of such an art deco building, but is not included on INBA's heritage list. The construction is in a very poor state of repair due to its age and lack of maintenance. This apartment building has polished black granite finishes and period, hand-forged ironwork. Its distinctive turquoise walls appear to be original features. The interior decoration is also notable for the simple, well-defined elements, geometrical ornamental touches, and a stylization of common shapes.

The façade is remarkable for the dynamic and large span of its surfaces, and its canopies decorated with prefabricated medallions and fretwork, a variety of textures and patterns on the finishes, and an interesting rhythm and geometry in the ironwork.

The interior residential spaces also have art deco features in the floor tiles, ceilings, and plasterwork moldings on the ceilings and, in some cases, the door moldings and knobs and bathroom furnishings. Similarly to this building, much of this architectural heritage was lost during the frenzied transformations of the city over the course of the 20th century. However, a sufficient number of highly prized examples can still be found today, making this part of the city a freely accessible art deco museum.

---

## LEARNINGS

If we begin by building up trust and consensual alternatives, we could innovate significantly with the approach to displacing the current occupants, desplazamiento, spatial variation, and densification, as outlined in our Neighborhood Housing Trust proposal.

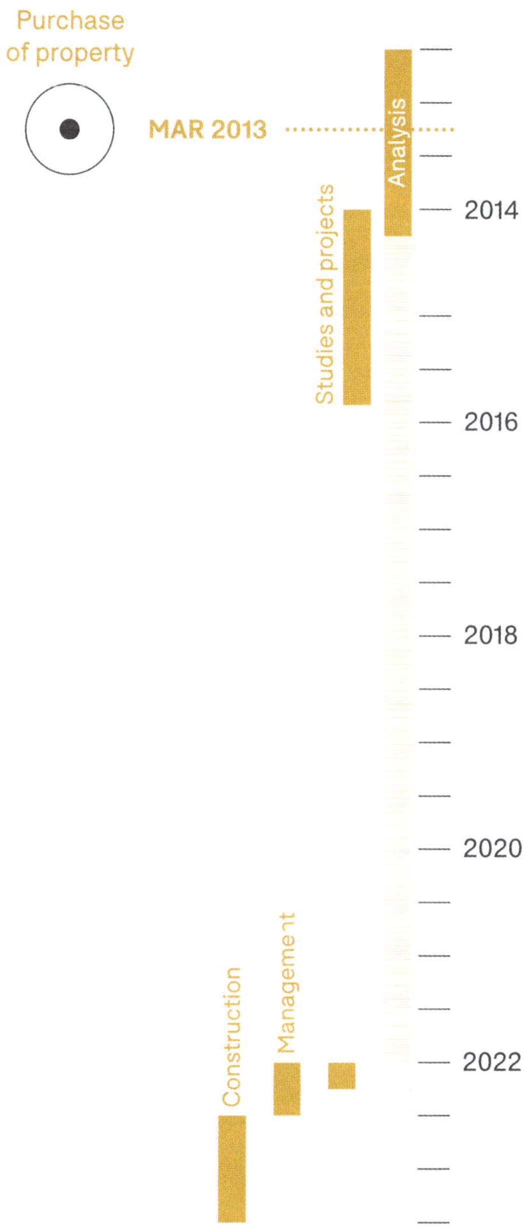
Purchase
of property
MAR 2013
Analysis
Studies and projects
2014
2016
2018
2020
Construction
Management
2022

# Zamora 15

Location
Zamora 15
Colonia Condesa

Distance to public space
800 meters,
Parque España

Distance to public transport station
350 meters,
M Chapultepec

Parking spaces
8

Year
2015 - Under construction

Heritage list
INBAL

Record of previous uses
Residential

Current use
Commercial + Offices + Residential

Percentage / $m^2$ recovered:
75% / 1,354 $m^2$

Partner architect
Eduardo Pesquera y Asociados

The current abandonment of buildings in Mexico City has become a primarily social and cultural problem that causes conflict due to the resulting insecurity and trespassing, as well as the loss of beneficial spaces for urban development and use. Works of significant historical importance are housed in constructions that reflect the city's history. These buildings, which should be in a different physical state, are often in a regrettably dilapidated condition.

This project's main objective is to rescue a set of six listed buildings in the Condesa neighborhood, in an intervention to restore the exterior rooms of the listed buildings with minimal interior changes.

The new housing project is placed within the plot (always in the background) leaving the ground floor almost completely free, except for the staircase and elevator wells, in order to maximize the amount of open space. On the upper levels, the construction's layout has a more open geometry to create different views over the city, with the most important one looking out toward the Chapultepec Castle.

In terms of its scale, the new volume, with its various views, is less connected to the series of listed buildings than to the city's distant horizons: it is related to the city's inner beltway (Circuito Interior) that passes nearby and to the height of the buildings on the other side of the Zamora and Agustín Melgar streets.

---

## RESULT AND IMPACT

Applying best practice and having a positive reputation can give you investment opportunities where you least expect them. For example, this project came to us after INBAL recommended us to the owners. From having a 14-story building, we collaborated with the local authorities and owners to create a 9-story building.

## LEARNINGS

Doing the right thing and following best urban practice (activated ground floors, mixed uses, open spaces) does not guarantee a direct and simple project.

The Zamora 15 timeline is indicative of the complexities of working in Mexico City, a reflection of decades of mistrust between citizens and the local authorities.

We learned the importance of having good partners and the right plot to ensure the resilience of a project.

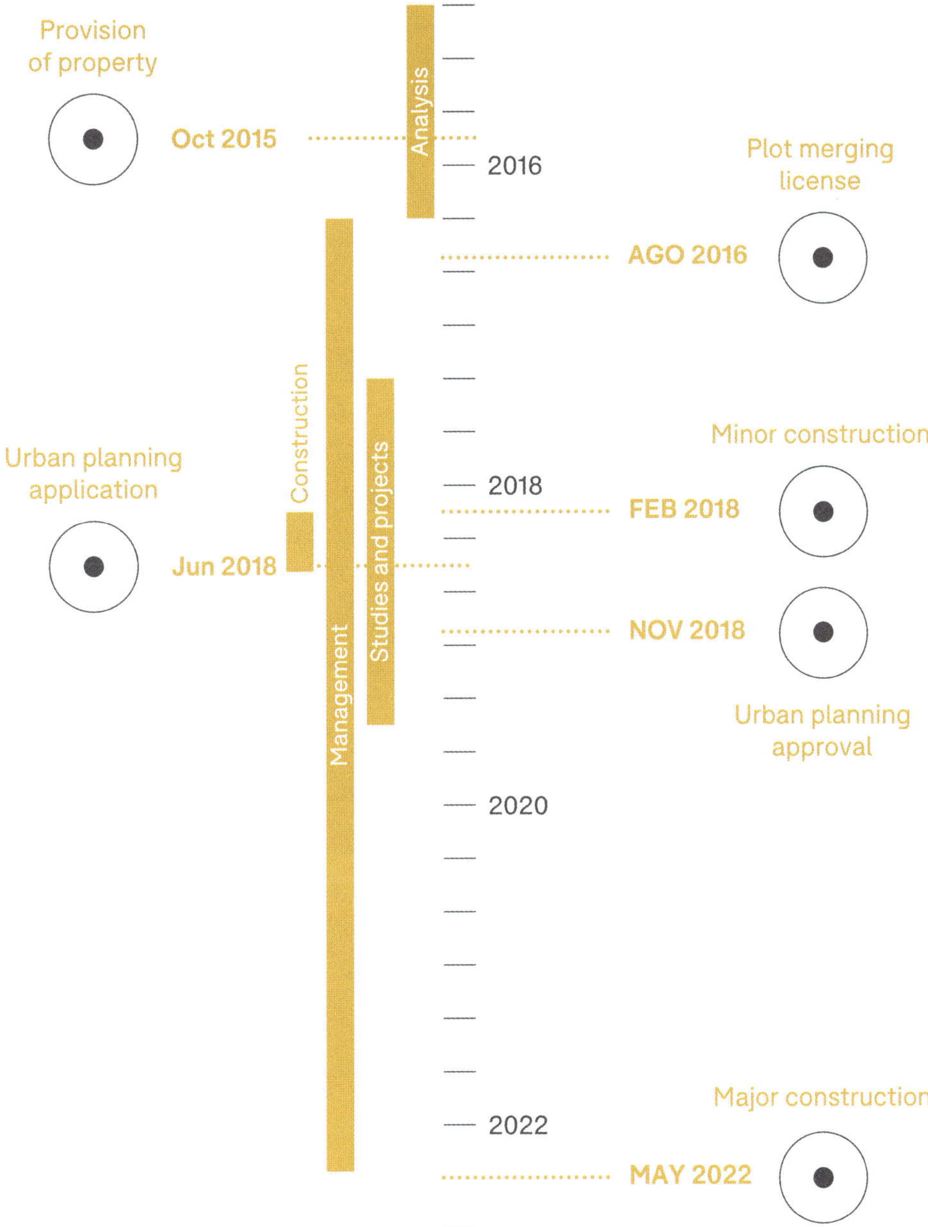

Provision of property
Oct 2015
Analysis
2016
Plot merging license
AGO 2016
Construction
Studies and projects
Management
Minor construction
2018
FEB 2018
Urban planning application
Jun 2018
NOV 2018
Urban planning approval
2020
Major construction
2022
MAY 2022

CAT

BBVA

# Further reflections

No More Inertia

Ideas on the City, Development, Regulations, and Architecture

On *Topes* and Logbooks

About, Profile, Who We Are, Philosophy, Manifesto, Mission, Vision

Manuel Dublán 46

# No More Inertia

Clara de Solà-Morales

Political motivation, legislation and planning give momentum to major changes to urban structures. These factors naturally define the city and will continue to do so. However, it would be reductionist and apathetic to consider this the only way forward. Such a mindset is also slightly antiquated.

In the best case scenarios, large cities implement policies of structural growth or renovation over decade-long cycles, targeting central areas or peripheries. Such large-scale projects are less about architecture or the urban form than connecting its parts to make a whole.

Cities are also defined by that muted mass that moves within pre-set parameters, by the construction and reconstruction of specially configured zones. And such a rewriting of the city is not only a stylistic exercise but an adaptation and an open and ongoing dialogue between the urban form, the city's changing uses, and ways of inhabiting it.

ReUrbano is a relevant and insightful actor in this rewriting process, through its choices of interventions and its proposed architectural typologies. Its importance also derives from the underlying analysis—on multiple overlapping scales—in each of its interventions.

It seems appropriate to view ReUrbano's rewriting as a change of grammatical style. In other words, instead of identifying and rescuing buildings whose importance lies in their location or architectural style, we should analyze their proposals for residential urban buildings' typologies: each project is a snippet view of their overall urban and architectural approach. Their typological proposals innovate the surrounding built environment and its positive effects on the urban context.

ReUrbano's residential developments are not the stereotypical family units of old; instead, they offer far more flexible and more contemporary methods of social interaction.

Living together is becoming less important. The buildings are not developed as a group of apartments but as urban and social entities with shared uses and spaces in mind: from communal courtyards and rooftops to laundry areas. These are the seeds of programmatic strategies being sown by ReUrbano (as part of a private housing project) through the discussion of pre-existing minimums and maximums in fledgling housing cooperatives.

# Ideas on the City, Development, Regulations, and Architecture

Juan Carral

1 Urban centers seem to be a non-renewable resource: we no longer have the *knowledge*, *capability* (or sometimes the *desire*) to build them. Historic centers are valuable because of their mix of history, urban memory, heritage architecture, public spaces, offer of services and trade, varied local populations, and different uses developed or developing over the years, the result of regulation and a financial perspective that is now different and seemingly impossible to reproduce.

2 Private-sector investments have created their own urban models, financed by a market that exists in a state of confusion and uncertainty. These investments have polarized the territory, and, backed by credit institutions, urban designers and academics, they have created a bland territory without making use of the available resources; such an impersonal, boring, exclusive and segregated approach does nothing to enhance public heritage.

3 Towering walls are a response to insecurity; monstrous roads built for cars seek to overcome distance. Communities only develop among people of similar financial status, education, and access to resources and information. Sometimes collective activities take place in private spaces. Heritage is rescued via institutional means by complying with regulations at the same time as jeopardizing the most marginalized sectors of Mexican society.

4 The private sector holds the keys to knowledge and professional practice. Meanwhile the government, despite its efforts to appear democratic, fair, and transparent, is increasingly remote, ineffective, overly complex and bureaucratic.

5 At the same time, some architecture is beginning to value intangible aspects that create a closer relation to the city, promoting accessibility, pushing the regulatory boundaries and challenging the typical, profit-oriented development model. This new approach focuses on renewing or replicating this neighborhood identity. It seems that design has a social and *civil* component that can have a powerful impact on cities.

6 In the early 21st century we are faced with a need to transform and build inclusive cities as never before. As architects and real-estate promoters, at whatever the scale (the bigger you are, the more complicated it becomes), we have the challenge of making buildings that promote inclusiveness or that make their ground floors welcoming to the city. We will need to conceive buildings with multiple products to generate a mixed community, from bedsits for students or single people to residences for families with one or two children.

7 More than ever, we must collaborate with local authorities; the initiative must come from the private sector but with ideas and actions that have a social impact. We must be faster, more agile, and increasingly effective to show to the government that working together will be the only way of sharing responsibilities and regenerating the urban fabric.

8 ReUrbano's work should set the standard for our cities, especially in provincial towns where constructions in urban centers have been replaced by developments in the suburbs in pursuit of questionable prosperity, short-term gains, and the irresponsible use of land.

# On *Topes* and Logbooks

## Diego Ricalde

The real and intensive occupation of spaces in Mexican cities is still far from being possible. The many examples of segregation and inaccessibility are as complex as they are obvious, as well as being frequently absurd and insulting. The problem is severe, and the solution is clearly beyond the reach of the praiseworthy yet superficial efforts made by government authorities, academics, and other professionals who are mainly focused on "improving" accessibility for differently abled people. Mexico City has a brand new name but the same old problems. Every day, whether we are in wheelchairs or not, we are confronted with countless barriers that fragment the city and the continuity of spatial experiences as found in vibrant urban centers with respectful and dignified architecture. In the Mexican capital (the world's second-largest city in terms of its size, and with the eighth-largest economy) it is very common and even dangerously normalized to find corners, sidewalks, streets, entrances, public transport, plazas, and buildings that were clearly not properly thought out. At least not for people who get around "on foot," "in a wheelchair," or "in any other kind of way because they can't afford a car or at least pretend to be able to." However, the problem goes much deeper and is far darker.

Some years ago, while driving in a country in old, well-off Europe, along a perfectly paved street without any high or low reliefs, one of my colleagues told me, indirectly referring to our country, that the number of road humps or *topes* was directly proportional to the health of its democracy. It is a bitter truth that the countless *topes* in Mexico City and across the country faithfully reflect our reality. Even in areas where government authorities have a degree of involvement, these *topes* are the protagonists in the ongoing urban tragedy that makes our cities, infrastructure and territories inaccessible. Another clear example of our lack of democracy and the untold impossible occupations of our spaces—less related to the urban space yet just as real—are the strangely confrontational visitor logbooks that are invariably a part of the landscape of every reception desk in public and private buildings. These omnipresent ledgers which, in exchange for a piece of ID and filling out a few boxes, give us the dubious privilege of owning a badge "to access" a space after we have sacrificed our dignity and fundamental right to be considered innocent until proven guilty. The spatial simulation of democracy and fairness reaches the most corrupt and insulting extremes in some centers of racial recognition disguised as shopping malls or "world-class" parks, in consumer centers disguised as "cultural corridors" or public transport hubs; simulations of public space, accepted and celebrated by the few, where spatial continuity and the right to the city are interrupted by barriers that are not necessarily physical or administrative but based on class, budget, race, and perhaps even caste.

We must want to understand and accept that we need more than ramps on sidewalks to overcome these *topes*, logbooks, and the discomfort caused by the many and daily examples of snobbism, discrimination, alienation, and despotism. Regrettably, and in many different ways, everyone in Mexico City faces adverse and undeserved urban conditions and as a result, unconsciously and gradually, we have given up on our right to the city. We are all "users" and all the actions that help combat discontinuities and social separation are the necessary and urgent uses.

Architects and professionals interested in urban dynamics and who recognize the depths of these abysses understand the urgency of creating new visions, and alternative stances built upon the basis of imagination, curiosity, respect, inclusion, communication, and representativeness. They know that aesthetic responsibility does not go far enough and that cooperation and interdisciplinarity are the necessary mechanisms to create value chains that enable us to make significant responses to our ecological and urban woes as citizens. They all know (or at least suspect) that the complex formula that allows or at least tries to combine visions between residents, professionals, financial institutions, authorities, theory and practice, are prerequisites for a dynamic, inclusive, and genuinely democratic city.

ReUrbano's "recipe" seems to take this approach or something close to it. This collective's previous, current, and future projects are examples of the vision and tenacity required to set in motion a complex and rusty piece of machinery that for decades has forgotten all about public projects, the city and its citizens. Discreetly, and probably more discreetly than needed, ReUrbano's projects are not one-off developments bowing to the tyranny of the financial system and urban whitewashing. While coping with the many whims of investment capital and public authorities, this collective's apparently stubborn efforts are conceived as pieces of a jigsaw that will gradually be assembled over time. The firm is not only trying to bring about a positive transformation of an urban subset that already works as a new centrality, but to create a more inclusive experience of the city (at least in this virtual site), from various perspectives. ReUrbano's initiatives and attempts, its omissions, projects, enterprises, forums, and publications all show a permanent willingness that constantly looks beyond the physical building and real-estate development and toward rescuing and genuinely building the city, with a vision on a larger and better scale, where each project is just one part.

To create alternative perspectives, nothing is more important than recognizing reality. The current economic and political conditions, not exclusive to Mexico yet very obvious in our country and capital city, clearly indicate that neither the state nor private capital can find solutions on their own. ReUrbano's attempts show that well-informed, fair, and close cooperation between both is urgently needed to activate the forgotten and seized-up machinery that makes city-making and citizenship possible. Only when there is genuine democracy in terms of urban access, and when there is continuity in the space, spatiality, and experience at the level of the city (not of the street), will the inclusion discourse cease to be politically correct but unfeasible. Only in this way can architecture, design, and all the professional and intellectual tools of the trade lead to concepts, creations, and constructions of fairer, more inclusive, and continuous spaces. Spaces, constructions, and cities without potholes, *topes*, logbooks, barriers, and attitudes. Spaces where we will be able to begin living, thinking, and understanding that spatial quality can and must be a basic and universal human right.

# About, Profile, Who We Are, Philosophy, Manifesto, Mission, Vision

Willy González

"About, Profile, Who We Are, Philosophy, Manifesto, Mission, Vision" is a far cry from the descriptions of Mexico's largest real-estate developers.

experience
group
create
buildings
way
constant
level
team
investment
clients
dwelling
ideurban
innovation
business
count
success
roots
big
administration
inhabitants
integral
architecture
mexican
marketing
creation
want
high
quality
years
home
developers
services
service
investors
goods
purchase
medium
operation
city
life

# Manuel Dublán 46
## Productora

Images of the late-19th-century house in the historical neighborhood of Tacubaya, the location of Manuel Dublán 46.

1. Reassess pre-modern typologies.
2. Reuse architectural features.
3. Rescue spatial qualities.
4. Respect pre-existing vegetation.
5. Reintegrate original openings.
6. Rethink historical cornices.
7. Reinterpret layers of history.
8. Redefine the neighborhood context and densification.
9. Restore handcrafted elements.
10. Rebuild the pre-existing house.
11. Reprogram former circulations.
12. Recognize integral solutions (decoration-structure).
13. Recycle structural features.
14. Reorient the building toward green spaces.
15. Reestablish the relationship between interior and exterior.

# Acknowledgments

This book is dedicated to all those who believed in our project.

To Ximena, for her unconditional support. To my family, for always being there by my side.

To Rodrigo, for sharing his perspective on the city, contributing with his creativity and infinite energy to make changes happen. To Ingrid, for her guidance and wisdom.

To everyone who decided to create, expand, rebuild their projects in our buildings: Gaby and Lalo; Elena; Beto, Lalo, David and Santi; Don Ricardo, Fredy, Enrique, Bruno and Paola.

To all those who have formed a part of ReUrbano's team. They are at the heart of the creative process, from start to finish, from the idea to the building. Our achievements are thanks to you.

To Paola, for her dedication to this book. To Lulú, for her unwavering commitment. To Pam for her perseverance.

To every architect and urban designer: you are essential to our transformation process to give something better to the city. Thank you for every collaboration, each one a challenge, an exploration, and a learning process: Clara, Lalo, Pancho, Julio, José, Javier, Gabriela, Jorge, Fernanda, Wonne, Carlos, Abel, Víctor, Diego, Emmanuel, Ignacio, Jorge, Juan, Laura, Bobi, Alejandro, Rodrigo, Mauricio, Jan, David, Esben.

To our neighbors, who give vibrancy to the spaces and open their doors to us, giving us feedback: Claudia, Ricardo, Raquel, Rábano, Daniel, Fausto and Rodrigo; to all of you who had faith in just an idea.

To all the investors who placed their trust in us and made it possible for us to go ahead with our project.

And finally, to those whose hands materialize our ideas: in particular Adán and Pancho, in representation of all the master builders, craftsmen, providers, construction workers, plumbers, electricians, odd-jobbers, night watchmen, security personnel. Everyone has left their mark.

This book is for the city that inspired it.

Thank you.

Alberto Kritzler

To Mateo, Diego, and Pablo...

I would like to express my thanks to everyone who has accompanied me on this journey, especially to Mara for her wisdom, patience, and presence by my side every day.

To Beto, for his trust, time, commitment, and friendship, all of which has made these years of hard work fun, as well as a constant and profound learning process.

To my mother, for her blind faith, my father for his example and guidance, and to Alonso for this friendship and loyalty. To everyone for their constant support, without questioning my work, fully trusting in my proposals from day one. Christel, Hugo, thank you also for joining in this endeavor.

To all the architects, colleagues, and teachers with whom I have had the honor of working and creating partnerships that have taught me so much; in particular, thank you Lalo for always motivating me.

To our investors, who placed their trust in us, helping us develop this initiative and showing confidence that we could make a change despite material challenges.

And finally, my thanks to the entire ReUrbano team, past and present, whose commitment and dedication have made it possible for us to do things differently. I hope that they feel as proud as I do.

Rodrigo Rivero-Borrell

# Contributors

ALBERTO KRITZLER
Graduated as an industrial engineer from the UIA. MBA from Stanford University in California. Co-founding partner of ReUrbano. Committee member of CoRe. Currently ReUrbano's Advisory Board Director.

ANDRÉS SAÑUDO
Graduated as an applied mathematician from the ITAM. Master's degree in International Real Estate and Planning from University College London. Committee member of CoRe. Currently ReUrbano's Coordinator of Social and Sustainable Public Policies and Development.

CLARA DE SOLÀ-MORALES
Graduated as an architect from the ETSAB, UPC in Barcelona. Master's degree in Architecture from the University of Harvard in Boston and currently studying a PhD at the ETSAB, UPC. Co-founding partner of Cadaval & Solà Morales. Clara works on research and housing projects.

DIEGO RICALDE
Graduated as an architect from the UNAM. Master's degree in Architecture and Urbanism from the Architectural Association in London. Co-founding partner of Estudio MMX, an architecture studio focused on design processes for all territorial scales. Faculty member of the "Cátedra Blanca" chair at the UIA.

GABRIELA ETCHEGARAY
Graduated as an architect from the UIA. Master's degree in Critical, Curatorial and Conceptual Practices from Columbia University in New York. Co-founding partner of Ambrosi Etchegaray. Founding partner of LAYA, a place, medium and space to express theoretical, mediatic, artistic and discursive proposals free from the domain and/or traditional expectations that promote a limited vision of architecture.

JORGE AMBROSI
Graduated as an architect from the UNAM. Jorge has developed numerous real-estate promotion and housing projects. Co-founding partner of Ambrosi Etchegaray. Faculty member of Columbia University in New York and CENTRO in Mexico City (Master's programs). Currently a member of Mexico's National System of Art Creators.

JUAN CARRAL
Graduated as an architect from the UNAM. Master's degree from the 21st Century Housing Laboratory from ETSAB, UPC in Barcelona. Founder of Juan Carral Arquitectura, a Cancun-based architecture studio that develops housing and urbanism projects.

PAOLA TOVAR
Graduated as an architect from the UNAM. Committee member of CoRe. Paola has developed several masterplans and managed large-scale projects, frequently working in conjunction with government authorities and multidisciplinary teams. Currently ReUrbano's Head of the Impact and Design Committee.

PRODUCTORA
A Mexico City-based architecture firm whose members include Abel Perles, Carlos Bedoya, Víctor Jaime, and Wonne Ickx—who are also promoters of LIGA, Space for Architecture.

RODRIGO RIVERO BORRELL
Graduated as an architect from the UNAM. Master's degree from the International University of Catalunya in Barcelona. Founding partner of ReUrbano. Committee member of CoRe, a civil association that develops public policy initiatives. Currently CEO of ReUrbano.

WILLY GONZÁLEZ
Graduated as an architect from the UIA. Co-founding partner of APRDELESP, an architecture firm focused on researching space and processes of appropriation.

# Credits

## REURBANO'S TEAM

Alberto Kritzler
Andrés Sañudo
Paola Tovar
Rodrigo Rivero Borrell

### History of ReUrbano

Alberto Kritzler
Abigail García
Adán Díaz
Adolfo Callejas
Alberto Leal
Alejandra Reynoso
Alejandra Trujillo
Alejandro Artigas
Alejandro Díaz
Alejandro Pirrón
Alma Sánchez
Ana Guevara
Ana Larqué
Ana Sánchez
Andrea García-Cano
Andrés Gracia
Andrés Sañudo
Ángel García de Quevedo
Anita Ayala
Antonio Valadéz
Arelys Ramírez
Axel Arreaza
Begoña Fernández
Bianca Martin
Brenda Morelos
Camila Ferrier
Cecilia Garduño
Christophe Suberville
Cristhian Dávila
Daniel Patricio
Daniel Rojas
Daniela Hernández
Daniela Jiménez
Daniela Levy
Demetrio Espinoza
Diana Prado
Diego Solís
Eduardo Buenrostro
Eduardo Morales
Elena Durán
Elibeth Cruz
Estefania Arellano
Fabiola Torres
Francisco Brown
Francisco Hernández
Francisco Padilla
Gerardo Hernández
Gerardo Romo
Guadalupe Álvarez
Guadalupe Limón
Hugo Díaz
Irving Granillo
Ivette Arredondo
Jessica Flores
Jesús Alcántara
Joel Altamirano
Katarina Brunbäck
Katia César
Laura Sánchez
Liliana Amado
Lucía Junco
Lulú Cabello
Malú Butrón
Marco Ochoa
Mari Rodríguez
María Muñóz
María Pacheco
Markus Kritzler
Martina Duque
Maya Escudero
Megan Hernández
Michel Femat
Miguel Ángel Rodríguez
Miguel Carrión
Miriam Montes
Pablo Prado
Pamela Wheatley
Paola Tovar
Patricio Molina
Paulina Santoyo
Roberto Cruz
Rodrigo Gómez-Mont
Rodrigo Rivero-Borrell
Santiago Creixell
Sebastián Prats
Sergio Rojas
Sofía Morfín
Uriel Becker
Víctor Fernández
Ximena Santaolalla
Yuri León

## PHOTOGRAPHY

ALBERTO KRITZLER
pp. 26-bottom left, 27-top left, 27-bottom, 29-bottom, 36-bottom right, 37-bottom, 38, 39-top right, 39-bottom, 40-except top left, 41-top right, 41-bottom right, 48-bottom, 49-top left, 50-top right, 51-bottom right, 59-right, 60-bottom right, 61-bottom, 67-top left, 69-center right, 70-top, 88-top, 89-except center right, 90-center, 107-bottom, 111-bottom, 125-bottom left, 135, 141-center left, 141-bottom, 175-center left, 182-bottom right, 196-199, 211-top left, 218-bottom right, 225-bottom left, 265-top left, 270-bottom left, 286-top right, 292-bottom left.

AKI ITAMI
pp. 123-top, 123-bottom left, 123-top right, 180-181, 225-except bottom left.

ARCHIVO REURBANO
pp. 30-top right, 31-bottom left, 57-bottom, 105-top, 105-center, 109-center left, 109-bottom left, 110-except top right, 113, 125-center, 132-133, 146, 183-top right, 188-189, 210, 224-bottom, 232-233, 234-right, 240-241, 243-center left, 243-bottom left, 256-bottom, 257, 262-263, 270-top, 278-center, 279-bottom left, 291-top right, 292-center.

ARQUINE
p. 109-bottom right.

ARTURO ARRIETA
pp. 16-19, 20-except top right, 21-except right, 66-except center right, 67-except top left, 68-except top left, 69-center left, 70-bottom, 71-bottom right, 76-77, 78-except top left, 79-except bottom right, 80-except bottom right, 81-except top left, 86-87, 88-bottom left, 89-center right, 90-except center, 91-left, 91-bottom.

BAUART
pp. 216-217.

DIANA ARNAU
pp. 104, 105-bottom, 125-top left, 226-227, 264, 265-except top left.

EMMANUEL MUN
p. 109-center right.

FRANK CARRERA
pp. 109-top, 111-center right, 125-top right, 224-top.

GERARDO SANDOVAL
pp. 20-top right, 26-right, 27-top right, 28, 29-center right, 30-bottom right, 31-except bottom left, 36-bottom left, 37-top right, 39-top left, 41-bottom left, 46-except top left, 47-center right, 48-center, 49-right, 50-top left, 50-bottom right, 51-bottom left, 56-except bottom left, 57-top, 58, 59-left, 60-top left, 60-bottom left, 61-top right, 66-center right, 68-top left, 69-top, 69-bottom, 71-top right, 71-bottom left, 78-top left, 79-bottom right, 80-bottom right, 110-top right, 111-center left, 174, 175-top left, 175-center right, 204, 205-top, 211-except top left, 219-bottom, 242-right, 243-top left, 243-center right, 243-bottom right, 280-center, 281-top left, 281-top right, 281-center, 292-top left, 292-bottom right, 293-except bottom left.

PP. 123-CENTER,
123-bottom right, 242-top.

MENTES_ENRIQUE
R. AGUILAR
pp. 160-right, 161-bottom, 251-except bottom left.

MIGUEL DE GUZMÁN
pp. 190-191.

ONNIS LUQUE
pp. 160-left, 248-249, 250, 251-bottom left, 271-273.

OSCAR HERNÁNDEZ
pp. 278-top, 281-bottom left, 281-bottom right.

PABLO PRADO
pp. 111-top, 124, 125-bottom right, 141-top right, 141-center right, 242-left, 270-bottom right, 271, 278-bottom, 286-center left, 286-bottom, 287-bottom right.

PAOLA TOVAR
pp. 46-top left, 47-center left, 48-left, 49-bottom, 50-bottom left, 51-top right, 141-top left, 205-bottom, 243-top center, 243-top right.

PRODUCTORA
p. 305

RAFAEL GAMO
pp. 218-top, 218-bottom left, 219-top, 219-center.

SANDRA PÉREZ NIETO
pp. 122, 134, 182-top, 182-bottom left, 183-except top right.

SERGIO LÓPEZ
pp. 20-right, 26-top left, 29-top, 29- center left, 30-top left, 30-bottom left, 36-top, 37-top left, 37-center, 39-center, 40-top left, 41-top left, 47-top, 47-bottom, 48-top, 51-top left, 56-bottom left, 60-top right, 60-center, 61-top left, 71-top left, 81-top left, 88-bottom right, 91-right, 107-top, 161-top, 161-center, 175-top right, 175-bottom, 234-left, 235, 256-except bottom, 279-except bottom left, 280-top, 280-bottom, 286-top left, 286-center right, 287-top, 287-bottom left, 293-bottom left.

# Roundtable discussions

After ten years of promoting and consolidating urban regeneration processes through strategic interventions, ReUrbano is now assessing the future challenges for city-making. Several agents took part in this documented conversation, with a view to re-questioning, re-approaching, and re-energizing their work.

The roundtable discussions among ReUrbano's co-founders and guests provide an opportunity for them to exchange views freely. Contributions from various perspectives focus on the real-estate developer's role in city-making, and on the potential opportunities that public policy and regulations can provide. Subjects include projects' successes, limitations, and problems that affect promoters, institutions, and local residents in central parts of Mexico City. A series of questions seek to initiate and inspire ideas that might offer changes, solutions, and challenges in the absence of the state's commitment to dignified housing, society, and the urban territory under their authority.

ROUNDTABLE 01
Public policy and urban regulations. Participants: Jorge Ambrosi, Juan Carral, Gabriela Etchegaray, Gustavo Gómez Peltier, Pepe Islas, Alberto Kritzler, Verónica Martínez, Esben Neander, Rodrigo Rivero Borrell, Andrés Sañudo. Rapporteur of the roundtable, "Incentivos al deber ser" (Incentivizes for taking responsibility) by Gabriela Etchegaray and Marina Povedano.

ROUNDTABLE 02
Conscious urbanism, uses and users. Participants: Jorge Ambrosi, Fernanda Canales, Gabriela Etchegaray, Guillermo González, Alberto Kritzler, Diego Ricalde, Rodrigo Rivero Borrell, Javier Sánchez, Andrés Sañudo. Rapporteur of the roundtable, "Hacia una consciencia del espacio compartido" (Toward an awareness of shared space) by Gabriela Etchegaray and Marina Povedano.

ROUNDTABLE 03
Preservation and new meanings. Participants: Jorge Ambrosi, Carlos Bedoya, Gabriela Etchegaray, Víctor Jaime, Alberto Kritzler, Karla Niño de Rivera, Alberto Odériz, Víctor Rico, Rodrigo Rivero Borrell, Mauricio Rocha, Andrés Sañudo. Rapporteur of the roundtable, "Conservación y resistencia. La memoria como un motor de transformación" (Conservation and resistance: Memory as an engine of transformation) by Gabriela Etchegaray and Marina Povedano.

ROUNDTABLE 04
Generating value through design. Participants: Jorge Ambrosi, Loreta Castro, Gabriela Etchegaray, Emiliano Godoy, Alberto Kritzler, Rodrigo Rivero Borrell, Joanna Ruiz Galindo, Andrés Sañudo, Surella Segú. Rapporteur of the roundtable, "Los valores invisibles del diseño" (The invisible values of design) by Gabriela Etchegaray and Marina Povedano.

# Editor's note

We joined this project to analyze, articulate, and provide a structure for examining ReUrbano's work as urban developers, playing the role as internal and external stakeholder, observer, editor. This publication has developed out of a critical (non-prescriptive and non-affirmative) approach to real-estate development. Beyond any utopian ambitions, LAYA's contribution to this book has been to revisit ideas that are already accepted but that, in ReUrbano's hands, have been given greater scope. They have also created new meanings that have emerged, challenging the *status quo*, and, through their development and discussion in this book, they have helped build a network of urban awareness.

**REURBANO**
**TOWARD A CITY**

First edition, 2021
ISBN 978-607-9489-88-5


Ámsterdam 163 A
Colonia Hipódromo, 06100
Ciudad de México
arquine.com

REURBANO

TEXTS
Gabriela Etchegaray, Karina Zatarain, Juan Carral, Clara de Solà-Morales, Willy González, Productora, Diego Ricalde

CURATOR AND EDITOR
LAYA - Gabriela Etchegaray

EDITORIAL MANAGMENT
Castaña Arango, Paola Tovar

CONTENTS
Gabriela Etchegaray, Alberto Kritzler, Paola Tovar

INFOGRAPHICS AND ILLUSTRATIONS
Mauricio Garza

URBAN TEST (MAPS)
AMBROSI ETCHEGARAY, Jorge Ambrosi, Gabriela Etchegaray, Marcos Colin

PROJECT'S AXONOMETRIES
LANZA ATELIER, Isabel Abascal y Alessandro Arienzo

PHOTOGRAPHY
Listed on the photography credits page

DESIGN
Ápice | Maira Fragoso

ARQUINE

DIRECTOR
Miquel Adrià

EDITOR
Andrea Griborio

EDITORIAL MANAGEMENT
Brenda Soto

TRANSLATION AND COPY EDITING
Quentin Pope, Fionn Petch

PREPRESS
Víctor Vicuña

ReUrbano was printed and bound in November 2021 by Asia Pacific Offset in China. It was printed on 100 gsm IKPP paper and set in typefaces of the F37 Bolton family. The print run was 1,000 copies.